ANYONE CAN GET AN A+

How To Beat Procrastination, Reduce Stress And Improve Your Grades

GEETANJALI MUKHERJEE

Cover Design: Geetanjali Mukherjee

Also by Geetanjali Mukherjee

Seamus Heaney: Select Poems

From Auden to Yeats: Critical Analysis of 30 Selected Poems

Will The Real Albert Speer Please Stand Up? The Many Faces of Hitler's Architect

Illusions: A Collection of Poems

Creating Consensus: The Journey Towards Banning Cluster Munitions

ANYONE CAN GET AN A+

Table of Contents

Prologue

Meet Jason and Grace

Jason loves playing basketball, hanging out with his friends, listening to music and strumming his guitar. What he hates is school, especially history - with all those pesky dates and names of battles and events that took place hundreds of years ago. Why should he care what the causes of the First World War were, or when would he need to know the dates for the Battle of Waterloo?

His big dream - to get recruited to play college basketball, and eventually play professionally. Multiple choice quizzes and boring lectures were just a bump in the road towards his dream, a particularly annoying bump.

Recently, Jason is called into a meeting at school with the guidance counselor. She has a serious look on her face, while explaining to Jason that his consistent Ds in many of his classes are holding him back, and are going to interfere with his future career goals.

Jason argues, "I'm going for a basketball scholarship, so how does my GPA matter?"

"Colleges care about their academic standards - and most athletic scholarships require you to maintain at least a B- average. That means you need to really pull up your grades Jason". The counselor can't really be serious, can she?

"Yes, it's true. If you don't do something about your grades, you can forget about college, with or without basketball."

This is the wake-up call Jason needs, but to do what? It is not as if he hasn't tried. It's just that every time he sits down to study with his books, determined to finally get the essay for his class done, or to study for an upcoming test, despite his good intentions he finds the entire evening disappearing without progressing beyond a few pages of the chapter he is trying to read. His phone buzzes, and he gets distracted by answering texts from his friends. Then he realizes that he is hungry, and gets up for a snack. Few minutes later, as he is reading and highlighting important passages in the book, the phone rings, and the conversation ends up taking a while.

The evening proceeds in this manner. At the end of the night, he has many underlined or highlighted passages in the book. It is late, and he shuts his books with the feeling of having spent the entire evening studying. Jason gives himself credit - "at least I read through the whole chapter". The next day however, he can't remember a single word he has read, and tells himself, "I studied all evening and it was a complete waste of time. I don't think I'm good at taking tests".

He tells his guidance counselor, Ms. Jones this - that he is studying hard and still isn't making any progress. Ms. Jones doesn't seem to believe his excuses, but she doesn't really say anything. Instead, she gives him a book on how to study and do well in tests. "I think this book has some tips, why don't you try reading it and applying them?"

Jason is skeptical, but if it is really true that he needs to drastically improve his grades in order to get a basketball scholarship, he has to improve something other than his jump shot. It can't hurt to give it a try, he thinks to himself.

***

Grace is a quiet, shy girl. She loves reading, and can always be seen with her nose in a book. She gets the highest grades in creative writing and her essays are frequently read out in class by the teacher and passed around for the other students as an example of "model writing".

She secretly dreams not of being a writer, as everyone

naturally assumes she will be, but a doctor. She hopes to one day become a surgeon, and work for Doctors Without Borders. However, Grace has problems with quantitative classes, such as mathematics and science.

Grace's high school guidance counselor schedules a session with her, to discuss her career options after school. The guidance counselor, Ms. Jones, informs Grace that she can be confident of getting into one of the best liberal arts programs in the country, with her excellent grades and volunteer work at the local hospital. Ms. Jones, is therefore, surprised to hear Grace say, "Actually, Ms. Jones, I have been thinking of going pre-med."

Grace is a top student, but her math and science grades will have to improve dramatically if she wants to even consider the rigors of a pre-med program. Hearing this, Grace is crushed, seeing her dream of being a doctor ending just as it began.

"I really am not good at math and science. I love biology, but I can never quite get the hang of chemical equations or vectors. I don't think I have what it takes to be a doctor after all".

Ms. Jones, not wanting to completely crush Grace's dream of medical school, gives her a few books on improving study skills. "Why don't you give these a read - maybe some of the tips can help you. You still have a year or so to improve your grades in this area - why don't we re-evaluate then?"

Grace doesn't really think a few books can help her - especially as quantitative subjects just aren't her thing. "I should stick to what I'm good at - and become a journalist. Maybe I can report on wars in conflict-ridden countries, that is almost the same thing as being in Doctors Without Borders". Grace tries to convince herself that she doesn't mind too much giving up her dream, that she can just find another dream instead.

Introduction

I wrote this book for every student who has ever said to themselves, "I can't do this"; "I'm not good at ___"; "I am too stupid to learn". This book is for those students, who like Jason or Grace, feel that they just can't understand certain subjects, or who have given up even before they have begun, resigning themselves to poor grades, because they think that somehow they aren't 'smart' enough to do as well as their classmates.

I was always seen as a good student. In school I got prizes. At home I dutifully did my homework. I went to law school and did my Masters' at an Ivy League university. I mostly got straight-As. I was the poster child for the perfect student. In reality, I went through periods where I struggled a lot with my classes and schoolwork. In high school, I struggled with the math and science courses, frequently not understanding at least 80% of what the teacher said in class. I sometimes asked my friends for help with my homework, copying their answers because I had no idea how to even start working through it on my own. Sitting for tests was a nightmare, because they underscored how little I knew. I vividly remember the panic and shame I felt, as a formerly good student, on a particular physics unit test, where unable to solve almost every problem, I would write whatever little I knew, put down the formulae, and then leave large gaps in the answer booklet, hoping that I could come back to it and magically find inspiration. Of course I never did. I went through plenty of false starts, and even after I started to get the hang of the coursework, it took a while for the results to show in my grades. I used many of the approaches that I have outlined in this book, some by design, many others by accident.

Here's the thing – I don't think that bad grades in school are necessarily the result of being lazy and not wanting to put in the work. I believe that sitting through classes not understanding a word, day in and day out, makes us start to doubt ourselves. We think, I am not meant to do this. We avoid trying. It's scary, confronting our inadequacies and shortcomings, seeing in black and white that I am falling behind and don't really know what to do about it. Over and over in school and college, I had this feeling. Sometimes I got the hang of the course and got a good grade. Sometimes I didn't. To a large extent it felt like a gamble, although I did see that working hard changed the odds more consistently in my favor. But I didn't have a consistent set of principles that would always help me to do well no matter what course I took. And even while I was doing well, I was always stressed out, believing that maybe I would bomb the next exam and it would all fall apart.

I began to read many books and articles on a wide variety of subjects – psychology, neuroscience, improving productivity, overcoming procrastination and learning more effectively. I started to see patterns, and realized that the times I did well in school were when I put into practice the principles talked about in these books. I just didn't know I was doing so, which is why I wasn't always able to replicate my results. This book grew out of a notebook I kept to jot down the things I was learning, where I also chronicled my own past successes and failures in school, and tried to find out what had worked for me and why. After all, there were times when I had done incredibly well in school. In my final year of law school I got the highest grades in some of my classes, despite fighting a mysterious illness (later diagnosed as glandular fever). In graduate school, I got As in most of my courses, and was inducted to a national society of honor students in my field. And in high school when I was struggling with most of my subjects - I improved steadily, and obtained the highest grades in my school in the O-level equivalent exams.

I wrote this book because I wanted to share what I learned

with other students who may be going through similarly frustrating experiences in school. Knowing exactly what study strategies are effective, and which ones simply waste time, will help you to know what to focus your time on. I wrote this book because I don't really believe that there are any inherently "good" or "bad" students. Some of us stumble onto study habits that are more effective than others. In my case, the very next year after my spectacular performance in the board exams (equivalent of 10th grade in India or O-levels elsewhere), I struggled with a whole new set of subjects, and got distinctly average grades in most subjects, because I started to study sub-optimally, without even realizing it. When I read about the principles of learning and neuroscience that underlie most of the strategies in this book, I realized exactly why I went through those periods of peaks and valleys throughout my school life – whenever I worked with how my brain works best, I did really well. When I failed to apply these principles and studied haphazardly, without a plan, and without engaging my brain in the right way, I got average results. I still studied hard, but not in the most efficient manner.

Doing well in school isn't about spending all your time studying, or even about being exceptionally smart. It is really about building good study habits, being disciplined and willing to look at the areas where you are weak, and find ways to strengthen them - whether by asking for help, or putting in the time to learn it yourself. It also means making productive use of your time, doing focused work when you're supposed to be studying, and then relaxing properly when you're not. Breaks, fun activities and sports can all be scheduled around studying, and provided you have a strategic plan and follow it diligently, you can have a life and still do well in school. The next few chapters discuss these habits and thinking patterns, and then we return to the stories of Jason and Grace, and see whether they have managed to learn something that helps them with their study challenges.

If you are consistently doing poorly in class, and would like to do better, or have to get better grades to maintain your scholarship, or you need to get a good score on a standardized test, this book is for you. This book is also for parents; by knowing the best methods to study, tips that reduce study time by cutting out inefficient strategies, you can encourage your children (even if they are reluctant to hear your advice) that they can improve their grades, in any subject, without spending all their time glued to their desk. Incorporate these strategies and you will find it easier to give up your previous inefficient habits, beat chronic procrastination, reduce your overall stress levels and improve your grades, in some cases, dramatically.

Every strategy in this book is something I implemented myself, in some cases stumbling upon them by accident. Most of the advice here is also backed up by science - I have read dozens of books and articles trying to learn what are the best ways to improve one's learning habits. Some of these lessons are ones I learned the hard way, making mistakes and trying to be the perfect student. In many ways this is the book that I wish I had when I was a student.

I firmly believe that anyone can change their grades for the better, regardless of where you are currently, with the right mental attitude, and the right tools in your belt. Anyone can use these tactics to completely transform their grades and their experience of studying. I believe that anyone can master any subject, if they are motivated enough, and are willing to put in some time and effort. No matter what you may have been told by your teachers in the past, if you are willing to apply these principles, you don't need to let arbitrary labels about talent or ability stop you from pursuing any field of study or academic discipline. Not only can anyone get an A+, they can do it with a smile!

So without further ado, let's begin!

Chapter 1
Adopting The Right Attitude

"I am convinced that attitude is the key to success or failure in almost any of life's endeavors. Your attitude - your perspective, your outlook, how you feel about yourself, how you feel about other people - determines your priorities, your actions, your values. Your attitude determines how you interact with other people and how you interact with yourself."

— Carolyn Warner

Most of us have a tendency to think that our abilities are fixed - that we all have natural gifts and shortcomings, and that certain talents, like being good at art or athletics or arithmetic, are not available to everyone. If you're facing challenges in school, you, your parents or your teachers may attribute your less than ideal grades to ability or lack of it. You may decide that rather than trying and failing, you might as well stop trying.

Although we all have some limitations, we have many more choices and more ability to change ourselves than we may think. Simply by changing our approach, and committing to working at it, we can improve our innate abilities. By changing your attitudes and beliefs, learning some study skills, and applying yourself, you can dramatically improve your grades.

Tip #1

Develop The Right Mindset

School is a fascinating place. We attend school in order to grow and learn and receive an education, and yet many of us are judged and labeled, often in our first year, these labels sticking with us throughout our school experiences. Someone is good at drawing, someone else likes to write. Some students are seen as trouble-makers; others are not good at math or have no sports ability. While it is natural that those with innate talent or interest in an area should be encouraged, more often than not, school is a place where we go to find out what we "Can't Do". Whether explicit or not, these labels can stay with us for years, determining what we believe about ourselves, and what we try to achieve.

If you have spent many years thinking that you're not able to do something, or that you're bad at something, it can be difficult to suddenly change that belief. Maybe your teachers criticized your creative writing, marking it all over with red pen. Maybe you just never could remember dates in history, getting everything mixed up. Maybe the sight of all the symbols (what's with all that Greek anyway?) in mathematics makes you feel dizzy. Whatever your previous history with a particular subject, don't let it interfere with what you can accomplish in the present.

Unfortunately, there is a clear cultural message that most of us receive as well – that those who are smart can do things easily, and that they don't need to try. This myth is perpetuated in every arena – sports, business, and in the classroom. Some students are "smart", so they naturally know how to create computer programs or solve math problems or ace a history test. The ones who aren't so fortunate, may work hard and get good grades occasionally, but that doesn't make them smart, and it doesn't mean that they can be relied on to do it consistently. These kinds of ideas are also gender-specific – girls are often fed a very subtle message that they can't handle math and science courses. Most of us aren't told this very specifically by anyone, but it's a subtle cultural memo that at some point is covertly downloaded into our psyche. There are many brilliant women working hard in the STEM fields worldwide; however, they face immense psychological, emotional and physical hurdles that mean far fewer women enter these fields than they should.

A famous research study was conducted by psychologist Dr. Carol Dweck. She tested some ideas on learning and beliefs on a group of students. Two groups of students (randomly chosen) were given a test on some fairly difficult problems. After the test, one group was praised for how smart they were, while the other was praised for how hard they had worked. Then the two groups were given another test, but this time they had a choice - they could choose a harder test from which they could learn, or an easy one similar to the one they had just taken. The group that was praised for being smart chose mostly to take a test similar to the previous one; while 90% of the group complimented on their effort, chose to take the more difficult test. Both groups were then given another test, which was quite difficult. The group praised for being smart disliked the task, while the ones who were praised for their hard work enjoyed both the struggle and the learning opportunity given by this task.

Dr. Dweck hypothesized that the difference in the groups was due to their different mindsets - by praising one group for being smart, they chose to hold on to their 'smart' status by not wanting to pick a harder test and possibly do badly. Dweck called this the "fixed mindset" group. The other group focused on effort, and chose to try even harder the next time - they were exhibiting the "growth mindset".

I come from a background where everyone in my family is an engineer (except my mother, who has a Bachelors' in mathematics and an MBA from a top business school). It wasn't enough to get good grades in my family – it was almost a given –

you had to be extraordinary. I never really felt extraordinary – I got straight As for many years, but never really thought of myself as "smart"– I knew how hard I had to work for every single A. When I was unhappy or had bad teachers I stopped studying and did poorly. In high school when I chose to take science and computer programming, I was one of seven girls in a classroom full of boys, and it was palpably clear that we were expected to be the dummies. The teachers barely paid us any attention except to gossip about boys or pop culture. The boys laughed loudly whenever any of us made a mistake or asked questions, making it clear that we were expected to fail, and that even trying was futile. I would love to say that their attitude made me determined to prove them wrong – it didn't. I already believed that these subjects weren't my forte; I was forced by my parents to take them. But I wasn't the sort to give up easily, and so I doggedly plodded through my coursework, determined to get the best grades I could, given the circumstances. Even when I aced every exam and received the highest grades in school (and a record number of school prizes), I still didn't really believe that I was smart. I believed that I was lucky – that the questions I had prepared for had appeared on the exam. I knew how hard I had worked, and I still believed that only non-smart people had to work hard.

It's only recently that I have come to rethink the whole question of what it means to be smart. Does being able to effortlessly do something make you smart, or can intelligence be changed, improved? I now think that maybe we put too much emphasis on "being" something – smart, beautiful, talented; and too little on "doing" – challenging ourselves, learning something new, expanding our circles of knowledge and influence. Maybe it doesn't matter how smart you are or aren't, but how much you are willing to learn. More than ever, the world is changing incredibly rapidly. Already many of the things I learned in school are outdated. Most of us will change careers a few times in our lives, what we learn in school and college will become obsolete and we will need to upgrade our skills. We need to learn how to learn, how to adapt to our changing world. I firmly believe that those who will thrive are those who aren't wedded to this idea of who is smart and who isn't. Those who are willing to learn and try things will have the advantage.

Dweck's research shows that your innate ability and talent matters much less than whether you believe that you can improve on it (*growth mindset*) or that you are stuck with what you have (*fixed mindset*). You may not be able to change your genes or how much talent you innately possess, but everyone can grow their abilities if they choose to put in the effort.

This is, not coincidentally, the theme of most inspiring sports films - the underdog team rallies together and pulls out a victory at the last second. Remind yourself of your favorite inspiring person (real or fictional) the next time you start to think that you can't do something, or that you're too stupid, or that some subject is just too hard. You can do it, you're as smart as you need to be, and no subject is a match for the right attitude and hard work. This is the first tip in this book because it is the most important – learning study skills and doing well in school is like developing a muscle, there's always room for growth.

Tip #2

Don't Compare Yourself To Your Peers

A recent article in the New York Times describes how smart, talented and outwardly successful students are falling prey to depression and mental health issues, some even taking their own lives because they feel overwhelmed by the pressure to be perfect. According to an organization that spreads awareness about mental health issues among students, more than half of all college students have had suicidal thoughts, and 1 in 10 have seriously considered ending their life. Every year in the United States, approximately 1,100 college students commit suicide. These statistics are chilling, but what is worse is that they stem from feelings of isolation, of being alone, and of not being good enough compared to their peers. In an age when we are just a click away from knowing everything everyone is doing, we can't help but constantly compare ourselves to others and fall short in our own estimation.

All around us people are accomplishing incredible feats – starting companies, landing record deals, becoming internet celebrities. It's become pretty common to be intimidated by all the seemingly amazing things others can do, and to doubt ourselves. Sometimes it feels like anyone who isn't doing something out of the ordinary must be lacking in some way. In the New York Times article, the writer describes how a student contemplating suicide compared herself to her classmates and found herself lacking. "Friends' lives, as told through selfies, showed them having more fun, making more friends and going to better parties. Even the meals they posted to Instagram looked more delicious." Social media compounds our natural insecurities, showing us in glossy images and excited punctuation that exactly as we feared, those around us are living far more exciting and meaningful lives. And we start to think that this reflects poorly on us.

We compare ourselves to others, our friends and classmates. Someone loves to read books and aces every English test. Someone else is a math whiz, and never needs to study, just gets perfect grades. Maybe because some things seem so effortless for others, or maybe because we feel intimidated by seeing someone far more obviously talented than ourselves, we start to have this list of “Can’t Dos”, things that we think we simply cannot master, or things that someone else does so much better, so we think why should we even bother in the first place. We think we can’t play the piano, or learn math, or act in a play. We decide that reading Shakespeare is beyond us, or that French grammar is just way too complicated to get the hang of. And we give up, before we even tried.

The thing is, though, we don’t really know everything everyone is doing. We only see the perfect, happy, filtered images. We don’t see the struggles and mistakes and sacrifices; we see the end product, the moment of happiness, the rare triumph. And from that we assume the rest – this person is happier, prettier, more successful, and by extension, we aren’t good enough.

And make no mistake, most of us go to incredible lengths to preserve this image of perfection. When I was in high school, my peers would habitually exaggerate how hard they were working - telling me how they had already completed going over the syllabus several times, and how many hours they were studying. I believed them, and got nervous, and stepped up my own studying, thinking that the amount I was doing wasn't enough to pass the exams with good grades. I tried to imitate my classmates' habits, even though it was only much later that I realized that they hadn't exactly been telling me (or each other) the truth.

This peer pressure continued to affect me in college. Most of my classmates in my first year of college seemed to be focusing on partying and having a good time, bragging about how late they stayed out and how much they had to drink. Many turned up to classes perfectly attired and made-up, and I felt incredibly awkward and gauche in comparison. I was perpetually anxious that I was a social loser, because those around me seemed to have it all, and effortlessly. I may not have had their social ease, but I had come to college to expand my own horizons, and I did. I tried new things - acting in a play, singing in a rock gospel choir, briefly joining a Portuguese band for one memorable performance, and getting elected to office in the Student Union. The high school me would have been proud of all I achieved. But my college self, comparing myself to my peers, kept focusing on how I simply wasn't 'cool enough' or 'social enough'.

It's only much later that I realized how unproductive it was to compare myself with my peers – I came from a very different background, and I had different goals for my time there. I had already gone out of my comfort zone and accomplished a lot, and comparing to others only diminished that. As someone said, success isn't measured by what you achieve, it is measured by how far you have come from where you started.

When we look around us, or read about successful people, the primary message that comes across is how talented someone is, and how inevitable it was that they would succeed. Success is shown to us as a straight line, heading in one direction, up. There are no detours, no turn-arounds, no missteps allowed. Faced with intense competition for spots in top colleges, scholarships and jobs, in an increasingly less certain world, young people today face even greater pressure to have perfect resumes and transcripts. When you aren't allowed to fail, either due to the expectations of others or yourself, although it may seem like you are being pragmatic and focusing on how to succeed, you are actually making it that much harder for yourself.

In her influential book *Mindset*, renowned psychologist Carol Dweck describes research that shows that the way we approach learning makes a difference to how much we learn. Allow yourself to make mistakes, to stumble a little while you learn something new, and eventually, you can surpass someone who is incredibly bright but is too afraid to try something in which they might do badly and risk looking dumb. There are also some students who work hard, but put themselves under such intense pressure to succeed at all costs, they can end up burning out, or doing poorly simply because they succumbed to stress. In *The Pursuit of Perfect*, Harvard psychologist Professor Tal Ben-Shahar says that those with an overly perfectionist outlook have unrealistic ideas of success – believing that they can't afford to make any mistakes or show any weaknesses. They focus on the destination more than the journey. Someone who has a more realistic outlook on the other hand, sees failure as "an opportunity for receiving feedback. Because she isn't intensely afraid of failure, she can learn from it – when she fails at something, she...learns what set her back. She then tries again..." Doing something badly then is how we learn to do something well.

Culturally, the message most of us receive is that those who don't seem to falter and have it all together, those who seem to effortlessly float from one success to another, those people are the ones to be admired and emulated. Not only do you admire, you expect the same from yourself and feel crushed or defeated when you can't make that happen. The problem with this sort of thinking is that ironically, your own success can cause you to feel even more like a failure. If you succeed in school in a particular sport, you feel great about yourself. You are one of the top sportspersons in your school, and you are fêted. Then you go to an inter-school tournament – where suddenly there are many others like you. Where you are just ordinary. If you believe that you have to be the best in every environment, if you look around at the others and feel inferior (the "fixed mindset"), then the tournament will be a very stressful environment. You might not ever want to attend another tournament, preferring to stay at school where you are still the best.

If on the other hand you approach sports with the "growth mindset" (see tip #1), you will go to the tournament excited about playing against others who are also quite good, and looking forward to all that you could learn. You would realize that while you aren't the best, you can probably improve with effort, and maybe try to get some pointers from watching or talking to the others. Maybe you work hard and do much better in the next tournament. You could apply this attitude to any aspect of your life.

And what about those who accomplish everything effortlessly? Well, maybe they aren't challenging themselves, and they only stick to those things they are good at. Maybe they too would like to try something new, but they are afraid of not being good enough right away, so they don't even allow themselves to try, preferring to stick only to things they can do smoothly.

Looking at peers and how they do things may not necessarily be optimal. A little friendly rivalry doesn't hurt; in fact it can actually spur you on. However, if comparing to others is pulling you down, it does more harm than good. The smartest strategy sometimes means simply ignoring the others completely and doing what works for you. Instead of comparing yourself to what others around you are doing, focus on what you can do, what you're good at, or what is possible for you. It's important to stretch yourself and try hard, but not to look at others and beat yourself up because you think you don't compare well. The years of being a student are short; they go by in a flash. Would you rather spend your time pursuing things that matter to you, things that you have always been curious to explore, things that you may not necessarily be good at but would like to try; or would you prefer to be bound by the path chosen by others, wondering if you are measuring up to accomplishments that you haven't even asked yourself if you really care about? The poet Mary Oliver summed it up when she said, *"Tell me, what is it you plan to do with your one wild and precious life?"*

Tip #3

Focus On What You Can Control

There are many things in life that we cannot control – our family and home life, the teachers at school, having the most conducive environment to study in. Study skills books don't usually cover the other, sometimes hidden, aspects of being a student. Most books on studying seem to be written for students whose only focus is attending school and having fun. Yet, for many students that is not the case. You may have to have neat papers, and organized notes, but your life may be far from neat or organized. You could be holding down multiple part-time jobs, or maybe dealing with family members' or your own health or financial issues. Maybe you share a room with siblings and don't have a quiet place to study. In many cases, you may just be juggling a really full schedule, with demanding extra-curricular activities, a part-time job, or maybe you have other family responsibilities that leave you with far less time to study.

Many parents stress about whether their child has everything they could possibly need to do well at school (and in life). They think the right school or the perfect environment will ensure their child's success. However, no matter how good an institution may look on paper and despite the best intentions, the reality is that sometimes things are far from ideal. On the other hand, many parents can't give their children the education they would like to, for financial or other reasons. Of course, it is great to be able to have all the resources and help you can get, but what if for some reason you don't? The key is not to give in to believing that your circumstances will hold you back, because they don't have to. It would be nice to have "a room of one's own", but it isn't necessary for good grades. All you need is to decide whether you will let your circumstances determine what you can or can't do.

I went to one of the most prestigious schools in the city I grew up in, where most of my family members went before me. Yet I had the most insensitive and damaging teachers for most of my time there, and hated going to school. At some point, I just stopped trying to learn, and focused on just getting through each day. Just before high school, I moved cities and enrolled in a school that was the completely opposite in most ways, it was a wonderful school; but even there I didn't always understand or do well in many subjects, and sometimes we had a lot of turnover of teachers, which made it hard to learn. By this time I had learned to take my education in my own hands, and *I* decided whether or not I would understand something, not my teachers, or my environment. In some of my classes it was obvious to me that my teachers had decided that I would be relegated to barely passing grades. I even caught them smirking when I asked too many questions, as if to say, "Why try so hard when we know you're not going to accomplish very much?" I was determined to prove them wrong - I needed good grades to go to college and I believed that I could do better. I worked hard and received the highest grades in my school for my O-level equivalent exams, and got good enough grades in my school-leaving exams (equivalent to A-levels) to go to one of the top law schools in England.

Maybe you think that being able to overcome discouraging teachers or a difficult home life in order to get good grades is doable, but what can you do in the face of challenges that affect your ability to learn? What if your mind works so differently from everyone else that you are always behind your classmates? What if your brain finds it difficult to translate the letters and numbers that you see into words and problems? Dyslexia is a learning disorder that makes it difficult to read, spell, write or do math. You would think that being dyslexic would stop you from doing too well academically, and that it might even constrain the kinds of things you could study. In this case, however, you would be wrong. Some of the world's greatest scientists, inventors, artists and even writers suffered from dyslexia, but didn't let it stop them from accomplishing great things. A short list of famous dyslexics – Albert Einstein, Thomas Edison, Leonardo da Vinci, W.B. Yeats, Andy Warhol and Richard Branson – shows us that even a learning disorder cannot stop us from success, if we choose not to let it.

While researching this book, I came across the story of Kimberly Erskine, who is 93% hard of hearing (i.e. she can hear only 7% combined in both ears). She was born with a hearing impairment, but growing up in a family with "hearing" individuals, she didn't learn sign language, or attend schools for children with special needs. Despite the fact that far fewer deaf students even attend college, due to the various difficulties they have to overcome; Kimberly graduated with honors as a double major in English and Writing Arts.

Kimberly had to overcome several challenges to get through her classes. She says that at times she couldn't hear her Professors in class. "This definitely made my course work more challenging. I had to rely more on text and taking good notes, reading my books, and figuring out things on my own more. My parents were very supportive of my education and I think that helped a lot. I was the first one in my family to complete college and I was always encouraged to push myself to succeed." As I learned more about her, I realized that it was her inner determination to not let her deafness be an impairment of any sort that helped her succeed. Kimberly experimented with different hearing aids and technological solutions, even when they weren't always seamless or caused her to be teased at school. She didn't let herself slack off or make excuses, taking AP (Advanced Placement) and honors classes in high school. She also practiced hard at speech therapy, working on correcting her mistakes, which resulted in her getting commendations for her proficiency levels given her advanced level of hearing loss.

Kimberly's story made me realize that many of us have

challenges that are larger than we would wish for or believe we can handle, and it is easy to give in to excuses or blame the gods of fate and circumstance. School and adolescence are hard for anyone, and having to face those challenges with additional burdens, of health or family problems, can make us feel like giving up before we have even started. However, I really believe that you have more power than you think you do. Even though we may not have the power to change others, or our circumstances, we can focus on changing our own actions. Once we start to change our own beliefs, the environment responds. This quote always inspires me when I'm feeling defeated:

> When your determination changes, everything will begin to move in the direction you desire. The moment you resolve to be victorious, every nerve and fiber in your being will immediately orient itself toward your success. On the other hand, if you think, "This is never going to work out," then at that instant every cell in your being will be deflated and give up the fight.

During school when I struggled with how much I had to do, or felt that my efforts didn't seem to correlate with my results, I watched inspiring movies and read books that gave me courage. Something specific I remember reading that really inspired me was the following lines from the poem "Invictus" by W.E. Henley (also quoted in the movie of the same name, starring Morgan Freeman and Matt Damon):

> It matters not how strait the gate,
> How charged with punishments the scroll,
> I am the master of my fate:
> I am the captain of my soul.

The reality is that not everyone has the same advantages or circumstances in life, but most of us can do a lot with what we do have, if we have the determination to succeed. This is a great time historically to be a student, with lots of wonderful study materials available online, many for free. If there is something you want to learn, chances are that there are books, videos and even courses available that are perfectly tailor-made to teach you. Don't use others as an excuse to not achieve your goals. Whatever your current study-related challenges, there are plenty of tips and methods in this book that can help, if you commit to applying them. If you really want to improve your grades, don't let anyone or anything get in your way.

Tip #4

Take The Long View

Given that this book is about improving your grades and doing better at school, this next sentence may be surprising. Grades aren't everything. Sure, doing well in school gives you more options, and you may need good grades in certain subjects to pursue a path that is important to you. And I do believe that you can learn to master any subject that you're struggling with. However, just because you can study anything doesn't mean you should.

Many well-meaning parents put inordinate pressure on their children to excel academically, sometimes even deciding what subjects they should study, what grades are acceptable (and what aren't), and what their future career should be. It is important to work hard and to strive to be successful, but how that success is defined should be something that you get to define for yourself (while remaining open to helpful advice). And even when you do want to aim for certain goals, it is acceptable (even usual) to falter and take a detour on the path to your goals. A bad grade on one test or even doing badly in one year of school doesn't determine your whole future, even though sometimes it might feel like that. It's important to maintain perspective, to take the long view. Although it is surprisingly counter-intuitive, but over the long-term, you are more likely to be successful when you enjoy your subjects and give yourself room to improve organically. Hard work is important, but you don't want to cultivate an all-or-nothing belief, that anything less than perfect grades isn't acceptable.

I know we all feel the pressure to take courses that look good on our résumé, or will appeal to future employers. However, wherever possible, learning what we are genuinely interested in will make the studying a lot less painful and dare I say it, even enjoyable. Most of you won't have a chance to learn a lot of new things after you leave the cocoons of formal education, and even if you do, it will be fractured and disjointed. School and college are a great time to experiment, take a chance, learn something new. It doesn't feel like it when you are going through it – the stakes feel impossibly high. But trust me, it's far more so in the real world; so it is relatively easier to try something new at this point. At no other time can you freely dabble in anything that is really interesting or learn a completely new skill.

Even if you have made up your mind to major in a field with a set requirement of courses, you likely have a little bit of leeway in a few extra courses. Choose areas that you are genuinely interested in, even if they are not commercially very useful or quite different from your career path, you never know how they might be useful later. If you're an art history major, take a course on computer programming or game theory. If you're studying business, experiment with a class on social psychology or Ancient Greek philosophy. Allow some time for serendipity – perhaps attending interesting lectures outside your field, or reading popular non-fiction in different genres. Research shows that going outside of your field and gaining some knowledge in different disciplines can be a great source of insights and creative breakthroughs in your work. Even if you don't see how it can help you with your career, the course you take could prove interesting conversation fodder on a date or a job interview. It might also give you a different perspective on the topic of your major.

While I was in law school, I took a class in ethnic politics and political conflict, purely because the topic sounded interesting. Very few fellow law students took classes elsewhere in the University, and it might have seemed like I was pursuing a whim during my final year, right when I could afford it the least. However, that class was one of the best I ever took, the subject turned out to be quite complementary to some of my law courses and it helped me to improve my paper-writing skills. The paper I wrote in that class also formed the basis of my presentation at a conference and my first published journal article.

Being passionate about what you're studying - even though not always possible, should be something you feel at least occasionally. Being genuinely interested in something means you put in extra effort to master it, you do additional reading on your own, you watch a movie or documentary connected to the topic, you bring your enthusiasm to seminars and confidently discuss your opinions. Being good at something and making the effort to learn more about the subject, might lead to interesting opportunities that you hadn't considered before.

In law school, I knew I didn't want to specialize in corporate law, but wasn't clear on what to do instead. I took a course in international criminal law, and it opened up an entire vista of possibilities. My project partner, a year senior to me, passed on his enthusiasm for the topic to me, inviting me to interesting campus rallies on controversial issues and recommending good books. I got really interested, even borrowing graphic novels from my Professor, and reading every book I could take out from the library on the subject. I never read any of my law textbooks completely, except those for this class. I ended up getting two internships related to human rights and international law, writing articles and books on the topic as well as my graduate thesis. I also worked in this field for my first few years after graduation. You never know what interesting class could spark off a lifelong interest or even illustrious career.

On the other hand, how do you get yourself to work on subjects that you don't like at all or ones that you are bored by? Find a way to make your work interesting - focus on aspects of it that are interesting, or focus on what doing well in school can help you to achieve. Remember to find your own reasons, not those given by parents or teachers. Getting better at a subject also makes it far more interesting. Read popular books on the subject, to understand the wider context. For instance, physics taught in school can be very boring, but there are some popular science books that describe interesting aspects such as quantum theory and can make physics fascinating. Similarly, I read a book on astronomy that was so interesting it made me want to learn more about planets and stars, although I had never been remotely interested previously.

If you aren't good at what you have to learn, work on it till you're better, and you will like it more. Spend some time on your worst subjects, and as you improve, you will hate them less and less.

Learning some of the things we need to in school may not always help us in our future career, but how we approach this learning will. We live in a time when there is so much to learn, and the world is constantly changing. In our lifetime we will have to learn many new skills, either in our jobs or in order to get new jobs. How you approach this in school will stick with you and be your foundation. Even if you are struggling now, if you try to turn it around, the lessons of finding ways to make your studying more appealing will stand you in good stead later. Learning physics or geography may not be topics you will need to know for your future career, but learning how to learn these things will always be relevant.

Chapter 2
Nourishing Your Mind and Body

"How would your life be different if... You were conscious about the food you ate, the people you surround yourself with, and the media you watch, listen to, or read? Let today be the day... You pay attention to what you feed your mind, your body, and your life. Create a nourishing environment conducive to your growth and well-being today."

-- Steve Maraboli

The pace of life today is hectic. We all need to get a lot done, we are pulled in different directions, and for most of us, taking care of ourselves usually is the first to (temporarily) be sacrificed. We tell ourselves that just as soon as things slow down, and we have more time, we will make time to eat healthier, and get enough exercise and sleep. For now, it's a steady diet of chips and caffeine and late nights.

Research shows us that counter-intuitively, taking the time to replenish ourselves actually helps us work at peak capacity, and make the best use of our study time. We need to take good care of our mind and body - because it impacts how we learn.

Tip #5

Make Time for Renewal

When we are busy, it is tempting to think that we don't have time to take breaks, so we try to just power through and keep going. This is a state of mind I frequently find myself in. When I'm writing on deadline, or have a lot of work to do, I just wake up earlier, go to bed later, and decide that all fun activities and time-wasters can wait till I'm done with my work. I start to rely on whatever food is convenient, overdose on coffee and stop making time for exercise or anything physically relaxing. This seems practical on the surface, but is it?

The brain needs energy to work on, and it also needs breaks to work efficiently. If we don't give ourselves a break, it's like a phone running on low battery - it will keep warning us that it is running low, and suddenly switch off, often at the worst possible moment. The same thing can happen with our minds. As we push ourselves, we get tired and cranky, and what was taking us 20 minutes before will take an hour. We stare at the page or the screen, but we are unable to focus properly. And we end up taking a break to do something like check emails or Facebook because we are not able to focus properly.

This becomes a cycle - taking breaks and procrastinating, feeling guiltier about how little we got done, and telling ourselves that now we have to catch up. We see time linearly - there is so much work to do, so we need to spend a lot of time working. We see all time as equal. But in actuality - when you're tired you can waste time by being much slower, not being able to focus. You can also get stressed out, which impacts your work further, causing more stress – a vicious cycle. We can try to pick ourselves up with caffeine or sugary snacks, but that's a short-term fix and doesn't always do the trick. Taking breaks to play a videogame or surf online doesn't help either because it's not a real break, just a time filler, a lot like empty calories for the mind. I'm not suggesting you can never do those things, but they can't substitute real renewal, like a bag of chips can't really substitute a healthy meal.

The Science Behind Breaks

Even though it seems counter-intuitive, even when and especially when, you're really busy and have a lot to get through, research shows that taking proper breaks and taking good care of our body and mind actually makes us far more productive.

Scientific research into the way our brain works has determined that we have two modes or two states of thinking - one that focuses on something intently in order to understand it, like a camera zooming in to capture the details of an image (called the *focus mode*) and another that looks at whatever the brain is trying to understand or learn from different angles - like a camera zooming out and getting the whole image from a distance (called the *diffuse mode*). We need to use both these modes in order to learn and apply this learning to both projects and assessments.

When we put our attention to a problem or a chapter that we are reading, and try to understand it without getting distracted, we are focusing intently on the task. This is crucial to learning, and is the basis of most of the studying we do - writing up homework assignments, learning for a test. The more we focus, the more we imprint the material we are studying in our mind. However, this mode uses up a lot of energy, and we can't focus for long periods of time without a break. In many instances, we also find that we get stuck in the same thought processes, and continuing to focus on the task doesn't really make a difference. Insights, like a different way to approach a physics problem or structure your paper, usually come when your mind is wandering, when you're doing something completely unrelated to the task, i.e. when you activate the *diffuse mode*.

Taking Strategic Breaks

Switching from one task to the other can help to generate ideas, and so can taking a break - doing something completely different, maybe going for a walk, playing sports or even taking a nap. When our minds are doing something completely unrelated to the task that we need to get done, often we can get an insight into how all the pieces fit together, or we can understand something we were struggling with just before. This is the *diffuse mode* at work - pulling on connections in our minds between different things - giving us the big-picture perspective.

That's why when you're stuck on a problem, taking a break and doing something else, maybe working on some other subject, and then getting back to what you were doing - you may suddenly find it easier to tackle. Your brain has made some progress on the problem even while you were doing something else, and not consciously thought about it. This doesn't work however if you are doing something else, but still thinking or worrying about the task. While writing this book ironically, I went through a phase where I needed to complete a few sections by a deadline, and the harder the work was getting, the more stressed I got and stopped following the above advice on taking breaks. When I did take a physical break, like going to the gym, my mind couldn't shut off, and I was obsessing about how little work I was getting done, how I would blow my deadline and how badly my work was going. I couldn't get any perspective because I couldn't take a real break. This phenomenon is pretty common with professionals or students who when faced with a lot of work start to reduce and even eliminate any activity that renews you mentally. The longer you go without adequate breaks and relaxation, the harder it is to get a new perspective and access big-picture insights; you get overwrought and it can seem overwhelming to complete everything you need to do.

This is when you might need to take more and better quality breaks, do something that is going to really de-stress you (for me it is reading fiction by my favorite authors), and then you can get back to your work recharged. It could be a short nap, or going for a walk, or a quick game of basketball with friends. Maybe going out with some friends to eat a healthy meal. Schedule some time for fun things that you love to do, that you can look forward to.

You might be thinking - but won't all these breaks cut into my work? Not if you are strategic and a little disciplined about it. Put in some focused work while you are feeling fresh (whenever in your day that happens to be) and schedule your breaks for when you get tired. Start by working on difficult assignments like problem sets when you're feeling rested, and when you're tired or ready for a break, do the more mundane jobs like organizing your notes, or picking up books from the library. And strategically sprinkle your breaks in between your work sessions.

You don't need to study all night or till 3 am if you're organized and follow the advice in this book. In fact, when I'm rushing off somewhere and I know I only have a short time to get something done, I find it is easier to focus and do the work. When I tell myself I have to work all day, my mind rebels and starts looking for distractions. An old saying goes - "work expands so as to fill the time available for its completion". I'm not suggesting that you be a slacker and watch movies all day, but don't push yourself endlessly without quality breaks. Trust me, your mind and your work will thank you.

Create A Self-Renewing Cycle

While in the short-run, taking mini-breaks or switching tasks will help you to get back to your work with more energy, the best way to perform consistently at your best is to inculcate habits that work in favor of being more productive. Our body and mind can be quite amazing, but only if we treat them well. Getting enough rest, eating the right foods that give us energy and stimulate the brain and ensuring our body remains active and healthy not only benefits our overall health, actually makes studying and learning easier.

Tip #6

Ensure That You Get Enough Sleep

Studying is almost synonymous with all-nighters -- bleary-eyed with tiredness and lack of sleep, on your sixth cup of coffee, you are struggling to pound out that 15-page paper due at 9 am. Sounds familiar? Everyone has done it. Unfortunately, the latest scientific research on how our brain works shows that cramming all night for a test, and learning on chronic low levels of sleep, not only hampers our productivity in the short-term, it affects our memory in the long run - we cannot remember what we learned even a few weeks later.

As we sleep, our brains make sense of all the information that we gathered overnight; sorting, creating connections between concepts that we already understand. During cycles of deep or slow wave sleep, we "replay" the activity from the day, deciding what is important and what can be discarded, and then creating connections between the important information and the knowledge we already possess. Imagine that the things you've learned all day are a large bag of assorted nuts that baby squirrels gathered and brought back home. Now the Mama Squirrel has to sort all the different types of nuts and put them away in jars with labels, and write down the inventory of what was brought in that day. Now Mama Squirrel can't do all this while the baby squirrels run around - so they need to sit quietly and not disturb her. This is how the brain works too - unless you get sufficient sleep, what you're learning won't be consolidated, because it can only be done while our conscious processes are halted. You won't be able to remember what you need, or learn new things quite as fast if you're always sleep-deprived.

This is another reason why it's a good idea to spread your studying out over time, instead of concentrating it all over a few days or hours. If you learn a little of a subject at a time, it has time to be processed and stored in the right jar, and labeled for easy retrieval later when you need a snack, and have a specific craving for pistachios.

Studies even show that sleeping within four hours of learning a new skill is most effective. Sleep, especially the deep cycles of REM (rapid eye movement) sleep, when we dream, consolidates all the information processed through the day, throwing out anything that made faint impressions or that the brain deems irrelevant. This sort of house-keeping is important for everyone, but it is especially crucial when trying to create new skills or learn new subjects.

In recent years, research has found yet another reason why we need adequate and regular sleep. The brain generates toxin build-up, just like the rest of the body does. In the body, there is a specific system for getting rid of this waste, the lymphatic system, which works throughout the day to remove toxins. The brain's own cleaning department, the cerebrospinal fluid, can only perform its toxin removal tasks at night. Without this process, waste products builds up, which are harmful to brain cells and impair normal cognitive processing. This explains why on days when we don't get sufficient sleep, we feel increasingly sluggish and tired, and can't think as clearly.

One way to improve your learning and catch up on sleep is to have a short 20 - 40 minute nap. Taking a nap can be a powerful strategy to reboot the system when you're feeling particularly exhausted – something even corporate executives are slowly discovering - but we often feel guilty or silly taking a nap, maybe because naps remind us of being in kindergarten. I fought against taking a nap during the day for years - but lately I have started waking even earlier than I usually do - and in order to make the most of the time I have to write, sometimes if I can find the time and am home, I take a short nap (or just lie down for 20 minutes in a darkened room). It's quite refreshing and I can get back to my work recharged. Many famous creative people throughout history took short daily naps – William Faulkner, Ayn Rand, Buckminster Fuller and even Stephen King, probably because they too discovered that you can be even more creative if you're fully rested.

Tip #7

Stay Healthy Through Exercise

Unless you are involved in some form of sports or other regular physical activity, the hectic pace of classes, assignments and other activities can push out finding time to get to the gym or maintaining a regular exercise regimen. This is especially true if you were used to compulsory PE classes in school and find yourself in college no longer forced to go through hateful forms of group torture. Like many students in school, I didn't really have a preferred form of exercise, I didn't play any sports (not well anyway), and I only did the bare minimum in school sports activities, especially in the final years of school. I went to college and didn't realize that if I didn't schedule some physical activities, they just wouldn't happen. I had danced in high school, but my skill level seemed amateurish compared to the competitive college dance clubs, and I never really joined any of them. I tried doing ad-hoc things - going swimming or jogging a few times a week, and walked around campus a lot, which provided a basic level of exercise. But not having got into the habit of scheduling exercise, I would let it fall off my radar whenever I got busy.

I had even less time for exercise during my Masters' program, and even though I signed up for the gym, I only went for short durations, and that too not very often. It was only much later that I realized how important a regular exercise regimen is, not just for physical fitness, but for your overall mental health as well. Exercise helps you release endorphins, which contribute to your feeling of well-being. College (and even high school) can be pretty stressful, and if you don't have a way to release that stress, it can build up, at the very least affecting your ability to study. Personally, I have also at times struggled with feeling depressed, especially when isolating myself and studying or working very hard, during the times coincidentally that I was skimping on physical activity. Regular exercise keeps stress levels at a manageable level, helping you to feel much more in control of your life. Even something basic like a walk makes all the difference. I can feel my spirits lifting, feeling much better in just 30 minutes of walking outside.

Exercising is also a great way to take more breaks, and we often get our best insights while stepping away from what we are working on, and doing something completely different. I often find that I get my best ideas while dancing to fun music or going for a longish walk outside. In fact, recent research shows that when you are stuck, and looking for inspiration, exercise can help to unleash your creativity.

Studies also show that moderate to high intensive exercise, even a few times a week, helps increase cognitive abilities, especially for those who were previously inactive. Exercising, along with making you feel better, releases a protein called BDNF (Brain-Derived Neurotrophic Factor), which repairs memory neurons and also resets certain processes, helping to clear the clutter from your mind as it were. In other words, you are literally getting smarter while you work out, creating more connections and improving your memory.

Although it may seem to be time-consuming, regular forms of activity actually give us more energy and enable us to get more done. Entrepreneur Richard Branson stated in an interview that exercising helps him to increase his daily productivity by four extra hours.

If you really aren't sporty at all (like me), find something that you like enough to do a few times a week, or find several things and cycle between them. You can try lots of different things till you find something you like. If nothing appeals, you can walk outdoors or on a treadmill, and can even use the time to catch up on school reading or memorize flashcards. The point is to make sure that you make the time for exercise, treating it just as importantly as any class.

Tip #8

Eat To Nourish Your Brain

It's easy when you're studying long hours and busy with lots of other activities to pay little attention to food. You just pick up whatever's easy and quick and tastes good. Maybe you carry packets of chips and cookies with you, to munch when you're hungry. Maybe you like to pick up fast food or something tasty like fried noodles to eat after class. Who has time to spend on worrying about eating healthy? Plus, when you're on a tight budget, fast, quick, junk food tastes good and is easy on your wallet.

The problem is, over time, this can actually make you less effective as a student. When I was in college, I was completely responsible for my own meals for the first time. I knew how to cook only a few things, also I didn't always have time to make elaborate meals - I had lots of other things to do. I got into the habit of eating a lot of pasta and bread, with very few fruits and vegetables. Later in graduate school, tired from a long day of classes, meetings, hours at my part-time job, I would stop to pick up Chinese take-out or a slice of pizza very often on my way home. I also ate a lot of sugary snacks like cakes and chocolate biscuits, keeping some in my bag as an energy boost during the day when I got tired. I didn't realize it at the time, but my poor diet was affecting my energy levels, my mood, and my health. I gained weight and didn't feel good about myself. I fell sick often, suffering from prolonged colds and flu, catching anything that was going around. After I graduated, I was ill for a long time, and had to spend a lot of effort slowly improving my health.

Due to the challenges I faced myself, I did a lot of research on proper nutrition, and what I learned was really surprising. Research has shown that the food we eat can affect our energy levels, our ability to focus and concentrate, and even our mood.

Eating junk food like potato chips versus eating brown rice and grilled chicken sends different signals to our brain, and breaks down differently in our digestion, which affect our alertness, our focus and even influences our feelings of self-esteem and confidence.

When you eat food like bread or cake or pasta - instead of filling you up, it actually causes certain chemical reactions in your body signaling that you're hungry soon after eating. Sugary foods or those with simple carbs give you instant energy, but it doesn't last long, and then you find yourself crashing, needing another boost. You have something else starchy, and the cycle repeats itself. Certain foods, those with more whole grains and fiber, like oatmeal, release glucose (the fuel that powers our brain's processes, and many other functions in the body) much more slowly, allowing you to maintain a more steady level of energy and attentiveness.

The other surprising result is how important fresh fruits and vegetables are to your brain (and the rest of your body) functioning optimally. Your body needs a wide variety of nutrients, especially to fuel your study sessions. When I changed my diet to include lots more fresh, healthy foods, and minimized processed and junk foods, I started to feel more mentally clear, aside from other more obvious health benefits. As a welcome side-effect, I now rarely fall sick, and when I do feel a cold coming on, I just eat a few extra fruits, and I'm fine.

I know it's hard to make time to make a lot of healthy foods, and buying such foods ready-made are usually quite expensive. One easy way to include more healthy food - keep some fruit with you, like a chopped apple or grapes in a container. You can eat these as a snack instead of junk food. Also, baby carrots or cherry tomatoes make a great snack. Another easy option - make a breakfast smoothie - the options are endless. You can use regular milk, or soy or almond milk, chopped fruit like bananas or peaches or frozen berries (or anything that is easily available), some oats, and optional additions like nuts, flaxseeds and protein powder. Blend this and carry with you or have it straight away – it's a great source of nutrition and keeps you full for a while and is pretty easy to make. Other easy options include having a vegetable soup or a salad with one meal every day, and cutting out the worst forms of junk food.

Although this book isn't about food, and I'm hardly a nutrition expert, I do believe that some simple changes to what we eat can impact how we feel about ourselves and our productivity. Why not use any help we can get?

Tip #9

Cut Back on Caffeine and Hydrate

Many of us think of coffee (or other caffeinated drinks) when we think of studying; it is an iconic combination like peanut butter and jelly. I couldn't study without a fresh cup of coffee sitting right next to me at all times, even if it was past midnight. I could also drink a cup of coffee and go straight to sleep, in fact, sometimes I fell asleep while drinking my coffee. Late night study sessions in college didn't seem complete without the requisite cup of java.

In law school, I started making my own version of espresso shots - instant coffee in a cup with a tablespoon of hot water - with milk and sugar. It was an instant caffeine hit. I often had three or four of these while cramming late at night. I remember this tingling feeling, and palpitations in my chest, but that didn't really stop me downing the espressos. When these weren't enough, I learned a bad habit that many of my classmates apparently resorted to - caffeine pills. These were over-the-counter drugs available at the supermarket (they were kept on the shelf next to the aspirins) with high doses of caffeine, meant to keep you awake and going for hours. I took these in the weeks before my exams, thinking that it was normal to do this since many others were, and that this was the reality of what it took to get through final exams in law school.

I gave up the pills and shots before my final year, but my needing-to-drink-coffee-while-working habit stayed. During my Masters' program, I drank a lot of coffee, but no more than others, or so I thought. Our lounge had a coffee pot on at all times, and we were encouraged to pour it into to-go cups and take to classes or to the library. I probably had at least four cups of this incredibly strong and terrible tasting coffee daily, more if I had deadlines. One day, when I was incredibly stressed by a paper that was due the next day, I had a few too many cups of coffee one after the other. I was nowhere closer to completing the paper, and beginning to feel ill and have trouble breathing. I decided to go home and try to work on my paper there. When I got home, I just felt worse still, and had trouble breathing for a while. I just couldn't catch my breath, it felt like every intake of breath was a struggle. I called my boyfriend, who drove me to the hospital, where I waited for what felt like forever to be seen by a doctor, and even longer to get some medication. The whole time I kept wheezing, struggling to breathe. It was excruciating, nothing like I had ever experienced before. It turns out I was having an extended panic attack, brought on by too much stress and stimulation. The doctor recommended I stay off caffeine for a while, and reluctantly I switched to decaf. That day was a huge wake-up call for me. I never did grow out of the need for coffee when I work, but knowing that I could have a bad reaction, I try to limit my intake, and switch to green or herbal tea if I need to. I even recently went through a detox period where I refrained from all caffeine for a week. While most students may never get to the stage of caffeine overdose that I did, surviving on copious quantities of caffeine and sugary carbs are common (and unhealthy) ways to get through stressful study periods.

Although it may feel like drinking coffee can actually perk you up, caffeine inherently doesn't have the ability to give you an energy boost, it simply masks the symptoms of tiredness. Research shows that caffeine mostly boosts performance when you are doing something that is routine; it gives you enough wakefulness to complete such tasks. But for tasks that require concentration and focus, or for learning something new, it may only have mild benefits (although it does affect each person differently). You also start to develop a tolerance to it, needing more and more for the same boost as before.

If you are constantly tired, it is worth looking into why that is. Maybe you simply need to get enough rest, do your important and focus-intensive work during your peak energy hours and give your body the nutrition (and hydration) it needs. Although caffeine can temporarily boost flagging energy, by not addressing the underlying causes, we are actually exacerbating the problem. Too much caffeine intake ironically often goes hand in hand with dehydration. The problem is that many of us are slightly dehydrated chronically and don't even realize it. We count up the cups of tea or coffee and soda and convince ourselves we are fine; however, sugary sodas and caffeine actually detract from the amount of fluid we need. Studies have shown that sometimes when we are tired, and reach for yet another pick-me-up stimulant, we are actually simply dehydrated.

Drinking more water can boost our energy levels. The brain needs lots of water to be fully alert - and even mild dehydration can have some very serious side-effects, including excessive tiredness, and feeling like you're in a fog that you can't get out of. Research has shown that being dehydrated by just 2% impairs our performance in cognitive tasks that require focus, attention and memory skills. While you might be like me and swear by your favorite cup(s) of joe, I suggest at the very least ensuring that you are well-hydrated, and reducing the amount of your caffeine intake. Keep water with you when you're studying and just keep drinking. You can also try flavored waters and herbal teas. You may even find that you need far less caffeine to keep you alert.

Chapter 3
Organizing Your Study Life

"If you don't know where you are going, you'll end up someplace else."

-- Yogi Berra

Your papers and notes are strewn all around your desk, and in piles on the floor. You have so many things to remember, some of them slip out of your mind occasionally. Unfortunately, this happens usually at the worst possible time, when you forget something really important. You routinely spend 20 minutes searching for an important paper related to one of your classes or extra-curricular activities. You sit down to study, but don't always work on what's most urgent, because you aren't sure what you're really supposed to be doing at any time. You have a vague feeling of uneasiness that you pretend is just the stress of being in school, but maybe it's something else.

Developing better study habits actually starts even before you sit down to study. Although this comes easier to some than others, being organized and planning your work saves a lot of time, and can be the secret weapon of getting better grades without a significant increase in time investment.

Tip #10

Figure Out Your Study Goals

You picked up this book because you want to improve your grades in some manner. However, jumping in without a specific goal won't be very effective. Before you start studying, at the planning stage, take a few minutes to figure out the primary goal for every course or topic you're studying. This may seem obvious, but it's surprising how often we simply make assumptions without even articulating those assumptions to ourselves. After all, if you don't know exactly where you are heading, how will you know you've got there? Also, you will need to tailor your strategies to your goals.

First, figure out a general goal for each subject or upcoming exam. For instance, you may be simply looking to improve your score on a standardized test. Or you're interested in getting through your end of year exams in a particular subject with a good grade. Of course, you might have other goals along the way, but if you know what your primary goal really is, it's easier to focus your strategies. For each course assess what your target is. Put this in writing - and this can change - but keep updating it as you find yourself refining your target, so that it becomes a compass to come back to.

For instance, to score well on standardized tests, you need to know how to answer a specific type of question that is most likely to appear on the test, as well as be able to do well under test conditions. You might be able to eventually figure out how to solve a specific problem, but for a standardized test, speed is essential along with accuracy, so you might need to practice solving problems faster. This can also be made easier if you practice lots of sample exams, because the same kind of questions come up over and over, and you'll get used to solving those, giving you an edge during the test.

On the other hand, if your goal is to be able to have a conversation in the language you're learning, or pass an oral exam, then drilling verb lists isn't going to be the best tactic. You can instead have practice conversations with friends who speak the language, or try an online service. Alternatively, you can memorize some phrases, even entire short speeches, in your target language. You could also spend time watching TV shows and movies or listening to music in that language, to familiarize yourself with the language, sounds and accents. These strategies also would work great (and are more fun) if you're learning a language as a hobby - you can go at your own pace and develop a feel for the language. In fact, I learned my third language, Hindi, initially by watching Bollywood movies and reading billboards. It worked for me because at the time I was also studying Hindi in school at a beginner's level. Watching movies helped me to expand my vocabulary rapidly, and I could understand (and later speak) far better than I could read or write in the language. However, this only helped me till a certain stage in my language learning. Later, when I had to write essays and give exams in the language, I had to use more traditional methods of learning.

It is also helpful when planning your overall goals to determine how much time you have. You can initially set a short-term goal, as well as a longer-term goal. For instance, if you're studying for an end-of-year exam and have nine months to go, you can break up the next few months into shorter periods, with smaller goals that lead up to the bigger one. For instance, your first goal could be to do the reading and learn the topics, or understand how to solve problems that you find challenging. The next goal could be improving your essay-writing skills, or completing more problems in less time. Or more simply, you could set a grade goal for yourself, and slowly try to improve your grade. Break the goal down into targets for each month, and then each week, which you can add to your weekly and daily planning (see below). If you're working on improving a quantitative skill, its best to spread out your learning over the space of a few months, through a systematic plan. Step-by-step increasing your ability or knowledge, you can dramatically improve your skill level if you practice regularly (see chapter 7). By breaking up your primary goal, you feel less pressure to accomplish a lot overnight, and if you overshoot your goal, that's just a bonus.

Tip #11

Create a Weekly Plan

Forgetting Tasks and Assignments

Some of us think that we don't really need a plan - we will remember everything that is important. After all, I have homework due in microeconomics every week – don't really need to write that down, do I? And that big paper coming up, well it's been stressing me out for a while, so hardly likely to forget that. Why waste time when I could be actually doing work on planning?

Here's why. We think we are good at remembering, but we aren't. Crucial items fall off the radar. We forget to return or pick up an important library book. We meant to go to office hours with the TA, but we forgot. They may seem only small things, but niggling things that we fail to do can cause stress and add disruption to our life. And you might remember something crucial in the middle of doing something else. If you don't have a plan or a system for capturing important information, you will feel tempted to stop what you're doing and make that phone call right away, or send that email to your Professor. And you get distracted, and one thing leads to another, and an hour passes before you get back to what you're doing, losing important momentum.

Constrained By Our Working Memory

Scientific studies of the brain have shown that for most people, our *working memory* or the part of short-term memory that holds items that we are immediately processing in our mind is only able to remember four things at a time. This might seem impossibly short, but consider the last time you went grocery shopping without a list - it was hard to remember more than 4 or 5 items, and you came home and remembered - oh, I needed yogurt! This is because you were relying on your working memory to remember what you needed to pick up. The other option is to go row by row and think - do I need pasta sauce? What about cereal? As you know, that's an incredibly inefficient way to shop (not to mention bad for your waistline as you might end up picking up too many extra things you didn't need!).

Another interesting discovery from neuroscience (the science of learning about our brain and how it works) is that we are really bad at evaluating priorities in our heads. This is because prioritizing is an activity that takes up a lot of energy, and it is difficult to remember the tasks you need to do and prioritize them at the same time (again, due to the limited capacity of your working memory). We get distracted, or give incorrect weightage to tasks; for instance deciding to spend two hours reading an article on Tuesday for a seminar on Friday, and running out of time to work on an economics homework due on Wednesday in class. It may seem obvious now in what order to do the work, but when you're in the moment, everything can seem an equal priority. This is why sometimes we tend to get really stressed and overwhelmed with everything we have to do.

Fail to Plan, Plan to Fail

A simple but incredibly effective solution is to create a plan for the week. This is something I started to do fairly recently. Whenever you're feeling overwhelmed - just take out a sheet of paper, and create a rough plan of everything you need to get done. When you start to create a weekly plan on a regular basis, you will find you're not getting stressed or overwhelmed by your schoolwork. Just seeing your plan, even if it might change, or you realize that you have a lot of things to do, can make you feel calmer.

The other advantage to having a written plan is that you have something to use when plans change for some reason.

Perhaps your teacher announces a surprise test for the next class, so you need to add in time to study this evening and tomorrow for it. Or maybe a seminar is canceled, and you need to decide what assignment you can complete in the time that is freed up. Relying on our brain to just decide what to do when things change, which they invariably will, is a recipe for wasting time and leads to overlooking ways to utilize your time in the best way.

Make Time to Plan

Make your plan at the same time every week. Cal Newport, author and advice blogger, calls this a "Sunday Ritual". You can make it a Friday evening ritual or a Saturday ritual if that suits you better - just pick a date and time that you can commit to every week. You can even make it a recurring event in your calendar, with an alarm to remind you to do the plan.

How you create your plan is entirely up to you. You can create your plan on paper, in a notebook or electronically. I usually write the first draft of my plan on paper, especially when I have a lot of different things going on and I have to decide what the biggest priority items are and where to include them. Then I usually type up my plan into Evernote - my preferred method of storing all my planning notes. You can use any method that appeals to you - just make sure it is something that you find easy to use and will continue, and that it is not something you will lose right away. If you can't find your plan, then it's just as bad as not having one.

All you need to create your plan is your syllabus for each course, and your calendar. First make a quick list of all the assignments that are due in the following week, with their due dates and what you need to do for each. Then scan for bigger projects that are coming up - paper deadlines, tests, internship deadlines to apply for. It's really crucial to use your syllabus for planning, to check for potential problems, and plan ahead. For instance, "figure out if you are expecting to go on a planned ski trip right at the time of a midterm exam," warns Dr. Margaret Reese, a student mentor, since usually you cannot change the dates for tests and major papers. Ideally the larger deadlines would also be flagged in your calendar - if not, go ahead and put the due dates, and reminders for a week earlier, in your calendar. Depending on what your larger projects are, put the next step(s) on your plan for this week - as something to get to after all the work due earlier is completed. Maybe you can schedule an hour to brainstorm paper topics and do some preliminary research. Or go through the notes for your class and check that you have everything to study for that upcoming test. Maybe you can go ahead and start preparing a study guide. Or get some of your doubts clarified. Just scheduling a few hours to put in some time for the bigger projects early on, will mean far less stress closer to the deadline.

Ideally, you would also have a daily plan, something that you can look at before you sit down to study, so that you are working on what's most important. As things come up, you can make changes to the weekly plan, and even make notes for anything that you know you will need to get done the following week. If you usually do this in your current week's plan, make sure you use that as the basis of your new plan next time.

Tip #12

Create a Daily plan

Be Flexible and Efficient

Just like the weekly plan helps you keep track of your assignments, a daily plan helps to concretize it and follow through to make sure the assigned tasks for the week get done. Ask yourself: what am I doing today? Creating a list of everything you need to do, and everything you intend to do, helps to get it done. It's a small trick that can help to make much better use of your time. The list helps you know what to do at any time, and the system is flexible enough that you can revise your plan if needed.

Neuroscience tells us that the part of our brain that we access to keep track of things like what time our economics class is, and remembering to drop off the library books due today, is very limited and can only hold a few ideas in mind at any one time (see tip #11). You can probably remember only two to three of the things you were meant to do today, unless you have a very regularized schedule that hardly ever changes. If you now try to add changes to this schedule – let's say, instead of meeting your study group at 3 pm, you're now meeting at 4 pm, you need to keep in mind this new information. At the same time, you also need to figure out what to do in this new slot of time available. Chances are that you can't really think of anything, and end up spending the time checking email or on Facebook.

Having a list makes it easy to see what you have planned already, and easily make changes to this plan. If something takes less or more time than planned, you can be flexible and add or subtract tasks. If someone asks you to do something, you can look at your list and determine if you can accommodate their request. The list is also a subtle trick against procrastination – seeing in black and white what you are supposed to be doing makes it a lot harder to spend all your time on something unrelated; I have found that even when I don't explicitly refer constantly to my list, I am more productive just by writing one. Research shows that you can be much more effective at prioritizing by simply getting tasks out of your head and on to paper. Once you have things written down, you can compare them, or classify them according to types of tasks. If you have a lot of errands in one area of campus for instance, you should group them together and try to do them all at once to save time. Without planning, you might end up making four trips instead of one, or spend your morning on reading that isn't urgent instead of doing an assignment that is due soon. Once we get distracted or start working on something, it is hard to also make decisions about the best use of our time. The brain isn't great at planning and executing on tasks at the same time, so make it easier on yourself by separating the two, and do the hard work of planning beforehand.

Implement the Weekly Plan

Creating a daily to-do list doesn't need to be complicated – it can be as simple as writing in a pocket planner or notebook or even just a single sheet of paper that you keep with you. If you're so inclined, you could use the digital approach – there are lots of great apps that can help you create to-do lists and mark the date due, as well as organize according to different categories. Some of the ones that I have used and liked are Wunderlist, Todoist and my favorite, Evernote. Most apps also let you add reminders and alerts, so you could use those to remind you to work on specific assignments. It doesn't really matter what you use to create your list; the best planning tool is one that you will use daily.

So what goes on your daily list? Basically, the list is there to refer to, so that you know what to get done today, and where possible, plan when you will do it as well. Circumstances do tend to change; your study group time might change, or a teacher fails to show up and you have some extra time, or you end up catching up with a friend. It's important not to be too rigid. Again, this is where having a list helps, so that you can be flexible. If you know what the old plan was, it's easier to quickly make the changes on the plan itself, than to keep it all in your head and decide what to do.

Be realistic when making this list. It's tempting to put everything you think you might be able to do, or would like to do on your list, but if you regularly find yourself not being able to get to more than half of your list, you will stop using it. The plan is a tool to help you, not make you feel guilty every time you look at it.

You could also use the daily list to hold reminders for non-study related things, like things to pick-up or buy or people to call. I add what I'm planning to cook for dinner, because otherwise I tend to forget what I was thinking of, and I feel less stressed knowing the decision has been made. You can also add in non-school appointments like lunch with a friend or a yoga class.

You can make your list in the morning or the night before, and it will only take a couple of minutes. Take a look at your calendar and class schedule and add in pre-existing appointments. Then in the time remaining, from your weekly list decide what really needs to get done and when you can schedule it. You could also add in time for recurring tasks like practicing a musical instrument, or putting extra time on a subject that you're struggling with (see section 7). Some experts also suggest that you should decide what time you will stop working and schedule something fun if possible, so that you don't feel like you're working constantly. Breaks actually help you get more done, and knowing that you have an end point will motivate you to work faster.

Tip #13

Organize Your Paperwork

Is Organizing For You?

Have you seen that episode of The Big Bang Theory where Leonard mentions Sheldon's compulsive need to label everything - including the label-maker? When I thought about being organized, I thought only a certain kind of person obsessed about it - creating a perfect filing system, labeling everything, fussing when one paper was out of place. I used to really be the opposite kind of person - I had a big box in my closet to throw all my clothes into, and I found the next day's outfit by rummaging through and finding the least wrinkled or dirty item to wear. I also put all the paper that came towards me on piles on my desk, and when it started to overflow, I shoved the excess into another box under the bed. I would never admit it, but my appalling "system", if you could call it that, caused me to lose lots of important items, which only emerged again just when I no longer needed it.

Since then I have learned to be a lot more organized, and create systems that work without taking a lot of time to set up and maintain. One of the biggest time-wasters when sitting down to study is to not be able to find one's notes or the homework assignments or other relevant material. Although no one expects or needs you to be a neat freak or compulsive organizer, your material should be arranged in such a way that you can find everything you need within a couple of minutes.

A Simple Organization System

A simple solution is to have a binder (or document box) for every course - and you simply need to put every piece of paper related to that course in that box or folder as it comes in. This includes the class syllabus, assignments, notes, anything and everything. If you take your notes in class on the computer, if you like, you could print those notes and file them in this folder as well.

Similarly, keep a folder in your Documents folder on your laptop (or desktop computer / or flash drive) for each course. The most basic but effective digital organization system is to have one folder for each course and within it sub-folders for lectures notes, papers / projects and assignments. If this seems too complex or too much work to maintain, just put everything related to the class in its main folder. You will be surprised just how helpful it will be to even have this basic level of organization and how much hassle it can save you when working on projects and preparing for exams. I have to admit I often just saved important reference material in my main Documents folder, neglecting to create course-wise folders. Needless to say, I couldn't always remember to use all the material I found because it wasn't easily accessible in one place, and relying on my memory of what material I found wasn't always the most reliable or accurate.

Preparing Materials For Exams

If you have neatly organized all your notes taken through the semester, both physically and digitally, preparing for the exam is far less stressful. Each week after class or during short breaks in the day, review your notes quickly, to check for gaps in the material that you can fill, either yourself or by asking for help from a classmate. Waiting till a week before the exam puts unnecessary pressure on yourself and reduces the time available to actually review the material.

Before starting to review for the exam, take some time to check if past exam papers are available for your course. Also check for any sample exams the Professor may have posted, and save them in your course folder as well. Having all the material you need for revising in one folder or box, makes it easy to take it with you to the library or another study spot for revision.

Organize Your Personal Papers

Other than course-related material, you might have other important papers to organize as well. These might include bank statements, scholarship forms, agendas for upcoming meetings of your extra-curricular activities and brochures for events you want to attend on campus. Because these aren't always easy to categorize, they may tend to just get piled up in some general way, and you might find yourself unable to find something till the event is over, or get repeated emails from your school administration because you forgot to file an important form.

You need a system to keep all your personal documents in order as well. Start by making a list of the types of papers that you usually need to deal with, by grouping them into categories that are easy for you to remember. Maybe a variation on this theme would work for you: Bank (for all statements and other documents from your financial institution), Club (one for each club or organization that you are actively involved in), Events (for events that you want to attend, or for keeping papers related to such events after attending them) and School Admin (for any administrative documents such as forms). Add any additional categories that are appropriate, or perhaps just a miscellaneous one that holds things that you can't easily categorize. Just remember, a miscellaneous category can quickly become the only category if you aren't careful and start shoving everything in there.

Set aside a day each week, or a few minutes every day if feasible, to go through all the papers, flyers and physical mail that comes in, and file away (or put in appropriate folders for later filing) those papers that don't require immediate action, but simply need to be kept for possible reference (such as bank statements). Those papers that relate to some action needed, process them right away by adding the items to your weekly list. Examples might include returning a completed form to the Bursar's Office, or signing up for a talk on campus that sounds interesting. If anything relates to an event or deadline, add those to your calendar with a reminder for closer to the actual date.

If you only need to process 10 - 15 items at a time, it can be done easily and become part of your regular routine. Organizing and planning don't come immediately to mind when thinking about study skills, but it is an incredibly important skill to acquire. Losing important documents, failing to hand in the necessary forms, and stepping over piles of paper to find this week's reading assignment will add unnecessary and avoidable stress to your student life. Implement a few simple processes and you can spend more time on being more effective and having a lot more fun.

Chapter 4
Getting the Most From Your Study Time

"It's not enough to be busy, so are the ants. The question is, what are we busy about?"

— Henry David Thoreau

There is so much to do in a day, most of us resort to multitasking without thinking - we send off emails while waiting in line, keep up with our friends' lives while commuting, and respond to instant messages while we are in meetings or in class. In fact, we are so used to multitasking, it is almost impossible to not do more than one thing at a time. This is however, affecting the way our brains process information, and can have a severe impact on how we study.

Research shows that sessions of focused work can help us to learn deeper, retain what we are learning, and apply it to other situations and contexts. In contrast, when we multitask, we are unable to form deeper connections to the material, and spend more time studying, and accomplish less. In order to maximize your learning from the time you spend studying, this section is about finding ways to improve your focus, utilize your time better and leverage your environment to make it more conducive to learning.

Tip #14
Manage Distractions

The internet is great for increasing our knowledge and connectivity, but it is also full of distractions. If you have a smartphone, then any number of beeps and buzzes can distract you all day, not to mention the instant availability of endless videos, games and the fun of chatting with friends, and catching up via social media. Given all this, it is almost a miracle that anyone gets anything done! Studies have shown that each year the US economy loses $650 billion to lost productivity every year from employees spending time on Facebook, Twitter and Youtube while at work. An article stated that on average, college students spend 3 hours on social media. A recent study of first-year college students showed that students who spent more time on social media had lower GPAs. At the same time, social media helps us to connect to others, keep up with what's going on in the lives of our friends and the wider world, and can even help to land internships and jobs. How do we find a balance between being connected and informed, and getting our work done?

Why Multitasking Doesn't Work

Other than something that you "should do", why do you need to manage distractions? Experts who have studied the brain have discovered that although we love to think that we can multitask effectively, the truth is that we don't multitask; we only switch from one task to the other, doing neither of them well. As a New York Times article describing the science behind attention states, "every status update you read on Facebook, every tweet or text message you get from a friend, is competing for resources in your brain with important things", like figuring out how to complete a problem set, or choosing a topic for an upcoming paper. As previously mentioned in chapter 2, our mind has two modes, and we switch between them when we work. For tasks that require us to pay attention, such as reading a book, driving, listening to a voicemail – these tasks are done in the *focus* mode and can only be done by the brain one at a time. When we multitask, for example switching from writing a paper to checking our messages, in essence, we suspend the attention we were devoting to the first task, and switch it to the second. It is also more inefficient: studies show that if you are interrupted, it takes twice as long to complete the task, and introduces twice as many errors. Each time we switch, we lose the train of thought, and find it difficult to get back to where we were; after being distracted, it takes on average 23 minutes to get back on track. More disturbingly, the longer we work in a distracted manner, the harder it gets for us to focus when we do need to.

This may seem obvious - that we should focus on doing one thing at a time - but very often it isn't. Maybe you're studying at home, sitting on your sofa or at your dining table, and your roommate or sibling comes in and puts the TV on. It is your favorite show - so you watch out of the corner of your eye, and before you know it, you start laughing at the whether a certain book you need for a class is jokes and forget about your reading. You decide you really need to get your reading done, so you go up to your room to focus. After a few minutes, your phone buzzes with a message from your friend. You type in a quick reply and get back to your reading. Then you remember that you were supposed to check available at the library, so you open your browser and check. By the time you get back to your reading, you realize you can't remember a single word you've read.

I used to study sometimes with my friends outside our dorm on the grass, sunning ourselves while revising for our exams. It seemed really productive - we sat there for hours with our books open on our laps. However, every few minutes, we would look up to admire cute boys playing a spirited game of Frisbee just a few feet away, sometimes getting up to return an escaped Frisbee disc. Or we would talk to each other. Or get up to get a snack. This clearly wasn't the most productive way to revise, and yet many students around us were doing the same thing, congratulating themselves on getting a lot of "studying" done on a beautiful day when they would all rather be doing something else.

Working in Focused Mode

As we have already seen in chapter 2, the brain needs to switch on its *focus mode* to be able to concentrate fully on a task, whether it is solving a math problem, or understanding the causes of a historical event. When we get distracted or switch to another task, that focus shifts. Then when we try to get back to the original task – it takes some time before we can get back to the point we were at before. That is not to say that we should never take breaks – on the contrary, well-timed breaks can actually help us to find an answer to something when we are stuck (our *diffuse mode* kicks in and keeps working on the problem), and we often come back to our work refreshed. But constant distractions and interruptions disrupt the thinking process, so that we get less done, and the quality of what we do get done is affected. This means we can spend more time studying, but accomplish less – simply because we are distracted.

The other benefit of focusing without distractions is that we are more easily able to enter the *flow state* – a state where we are able to almost effortlessly focus on our work, when time flies and we are absorbed in what we are doing . This is what some athletes call being *in the zone*. Not only is studying much more enjoyable when we are working in the flow state, but research shows that learning is deeper in this state, and we are able to make connections between what we are studying, and other topics, which is also known as *transfer*.

Working Without Distractions

The best way to work with focus is to switch off your phone (or put it on silent or vibrate mode), and decide to work on a specific assignment (read an article, solve a problem set, take notes on a book chapter) for a specific length of time, without interruptions. Ideally, you would be working somewhere with fewer distractions, somewhere easy to focus, like the library. It helps to decide in advance what you'll be working on, and also how long. For instance, if you say to yourself, I will work on the math problems for 40 minutes, and then I can take a 10 minute break, then when you feel like checking your phone after half an hour, you can remind yourself that you only need to work for 10 more minutes, after which you can take a break.

You can also break up your work day into periods for different types of work. Some scientists and productive people suggest that it is more efficient to do work that requires blocks of focused thinking, such as writing a paper or preparing for a test, when your mind is fresh and you have no distractions. You can also schedule time in your day, perhaps when your energy is lower, to catch up on social media and email. Instead of being "always on", it is more effective to work in certain blocks with devices and notifications turned off, knowing that you will have a dedicated social media break later on.

By working in focused bursts, you can actually get more and better quality work done and complete your work faster, so that you can go ahead and take a break and catch up with friends or update your Instagram without feeling guilty or affecting your schoolwork.

Tip #15
Beware Pseudo-work

Are You Actually Working?

Every school and college library is full of students clearly not wanting to be there - staring at the same page in their book for half an hour, texting on their phone, or asleep with their books scattered about. They look like they are putting in long hours studying, but how effective are they really?

When I was in law school, every study table was piled high with notes and books, and the library was always packed. I used to feel intimidated, worrying about how much everyone was getting done and how hard they were working, especially because I would usually escape after a couple of hours. I mentioned this to one of my Professors, and she told me - "Don't be fooled - they waste at least half their time chatting and flirting". Cal Newport calls this doing *pseudo-work* - it may look like work, and you might be able to fool yourself, but really, you're not making any progress and simply wasting your time. Worse, you are convincing yourself that you're actually working very hard.

I'm writing part of this book at a reading room in my apartment complex, where students bring their homework to study. There's this student who comes in almost every day, parked on the same table with lots of papers and books, 'studying' for hours. In reality, he spends most of his time on his phone, calling his friends, texting, and just flipping through the pages of a book, only to get distracted by the next text message or phone call. Sure, it may be boring to be indoors studying when you would rather be having fun with your friends. Spending hours distracted and sort-of working isn't the solution however, it only makes you think you're studying really hard, without actually making much progress.

Stick To Your Plan

A better strategy is to make a specific plan (ideally, consult your weekly and daily plans -- see tips #11 and 12) for what you will get done during a study session. If you have a tendency to procrastinate, it could be that you simply don't have an effective strategy to handle it (see chapter 5 for more tips overcoming procrastination). Maybe you can break the work into smaller chunks - and work on one chunk at a time. Give yourself a short break - maybe check your messages real quick, or play a quick game - then get back to the next task. Use the Pomodoro method (see tip #21) if that helps. Even a short timed session on the tough assignment you're avoiding can move it forward, you end up realizing that it is not so bad, and by making progress you might end up feeling so good, that you get the energy to tackle something else.

Never just tell yourself that you'll "sit down to study" or "get work done". Pick a specific task. When I was studying for my Masters' degree, I never had too many free hours in a row - with my day broken up by classes, or my part-time job, or responsibility with the committees I was on. I always had a specific assignment in mind when I studied - a particular problem set or doing the reading for a particular seminar. That way you know exactly what you intend to do, and know when it's done. And you can take a legitimate break, knowing you've done the work you needed to, perhaps joining your friends on the basketball court or going out to dinner.

Take Regular Breaks

When you force yourself to work for long periods without a break, you end up being far less effective. After too long on one task, your energy starts to taper off, so subconsciously you start to slack off while ostensibly still 'working'. You are at the library, aren't you? How could it hurt to just check your email for a minute? Next thing you know, you have wasted 40 minutes. You are far better off either switching tasks, or simply deciding to call it quits, and going to the gym or out with a friend instead (see chapter 2 on why taking regular breaks helps you to be more productive). In order to be even more effective, plan when you will stop working before you start, then you have an endpoint to work towards. Also plan days or blocks of time when you won't work at all, giving you more incentive to get the work you need to done quicker.

This advice is easy to give and difficult to follow. I often find myself with a vague intention to 'work', without a specific plan on what I'm going to be working on. Also, I have an idea that I will work for a few hours, with no specifics. That's usually a recipe for procrastination – I put off working because I think I have to do a huge amount all at once, and I don't know exactly what I'm going to work on, and that subconsciously adds to my anxiety. A novelist who dramatically increased her daily output by almost five times, said that one of the big changes she made was planning what she was going to write. Planning ahead what you're going to study helps you to manage distractions, get right to work and improve your productivity in the time that you do spend studying.

Tip #16

Use Bits of Time

There's Never Enough Study Time

Raise your hand if this scenario is familiar: you have classes all day - with 40 – 60 minute intervals. You know that you have to spend some of that time walking to class, and have a quick lunch in the cafeteria during a longish break. You think to yourself - I couldn't possibly get any work done during these short breaks, and so you spend the time talking to friends, checking Facebook, looking at your email. You save all your 'real' studying for when classes end, and you can go to the library (or home) and work uninterrupted. When you do get down to study - you realize that you have three chapters to read, two problem sets, a short 3-page paper and the proposal for a 30-page paper, all due in the next couple of days, and start to feel overwhelmed. Where do you start? At this point dinner beckons. After dinner you finally sit down to work, and realize that you need a book from the reserved section of the library. Retrieving that book takes 45 minutes (it is in another building). By the time the evening is over, you manage to read one chapter, and you feel stressed thinking about how to make up the time the next day.

It's true - small gaps in your schedule peppered through the day make it hard to sit down and concentrate on getting certain kinds of work done - like writing a paper, or reading several articles for class. However, the more you get done during the day, there is less pressure to cram in all your work in the hours between the end of classes and going to bed, leaving some free time to eat dinner, not to mention needing to have some down time.

During the day is also when your brain is at its most awake and alert, when you can get a lot more done in less time, even in small chunks of time. This is especially true when you're working on something new and challenging; the harder something is, the shorter time intervals you can spend on it before feeling tired or getting distracted.

As the day goes on, you get more tired, your energy drops, and just focusing on the work takes more energy than you feel you have. Invariably, caffeine and sugar are what you reach for to keep awake and keep working, but these are temporary fixes and unhealthy over a longer period of time. In the evening there are also more distractions – friends dropping in or calling to hang out, favorite TV shows, family demands. Working in one long block of time also makes the work seem more overwhelming, and makes it easier to procrastinate.

Use Time Confetti

The solution: make better use of the time during the day (between and right after classes), when you are fresher, and leave less work to do at night, when you are far more tired and not at your best.

There are a few ways to do this. Firstly, if you only have very short breaks between classes, while you can't make significant headway on large assignments, there are several smaller tasks that you can complete if you plan in advance. When you are creating a weekly plan (see tip #11) of every assignment, or reading, that needs to get done during the week, at the same time, check to see if you have all the materials you need, for example the books and articles you need to read. Make a list of everything you might need to get - books from the reserve section, photocopies of relevant articles. These are jobs you can get done when you have a spare 30 - 45 minutes, saving you time later. Also, add other little study related errands such as returning books, checking and filling in gaps in your class notes or buying stationery supplies that you can get done in shorter breaks.

Also, make it a habit to carry your homework problem sets with you - and if you have more than an hour between classes, you can start to work on the problems. This has other benefits (see tip #27), but also uses up spare time that would otherwise just be wasted. Problems benefit from being looked at with a fresh mind - so are ideally suited for 40 - 60 minute bursts of attention. Maybe you only get two problems out of six done, but that's one-third of your assignment completed, before you even finish your classes for the day. This also works with short reading assignments.

If you tend to make flashcards to study for tests - you can use the little bits of time to create new flashcards for an upcoming test, making you more prepared and far less stressed. You could also check whether your class notes are up-to-date, and ask a friend to help fill in the gaps. If you use apps on your phone to review material - for language vocabulary, history facts, medical terminology or anything that requires memorization - you could spend 15 - 20 minutes on reviewing some material that you need to learn - using up those pesky minutes standing in line at the bank or post office, riding on the bus, or when you have a few minutes between other activities.

Making Good Use of Long Breaks

When you have longer breaks between classes, or those days when you have time before the first class, plan ahead and use this time to get started on homework, reading assignments, even research for a paper. If you break your projects up into smaller tasks (see tip #20), you could schedule one or more such tasks to complete during this time. Sandwiched between classes and other meetings, you could start to knock off your painful tasks one at a time without even feeling the pain of a tough project.

Some colleges and libraries have special facilities such as the availability of rooms or study carrels that can be booked or requested by students. In my university there were several rooms that were available to both undergraduates and graduate students at one of the libraries on campus. Although these rooms were in high demand, if you arrived early enough, you could usually get a room. I often planned my day to arrive on campus by 9 am, book one of these rooms, and set up my books and reading materials. The advantage of working here was the privacy and focus they provided. The rooms were pretty basic - a desk, a chair, a bookshelf, outlets to plug in your laptop and an ethernet cable. Because of the almost monastic simplicity of the rooms, it was easy to focus and just get to work (although I was lucky not to have a smartphone at the time, so couldn't distract myself with games or Facebook).

The advantage of the room at the library was that I could study till about fifteen minutes before my class, and return after the lecture finished to continue studying. This way I was able to use the time between lectures with no overhead of finding a place to work, time spent in setting up, bumping into friends and chatting. Even if this option isn't available, there are equally advantageous alternatives. You can go to a library or reading room that is less popular with your friends, so you aren't likely to be tempted to chat instead of working. Whatever spot you pick, you should be able to easily set up and get to work, so that more time is spent studying and not on finding the right environment.

Tip #17

Change Your Environment To Prevent Boredom

Work In A Conducive Environment

Your environment can affect the way you do your work, far more than you might think. Some environments are more conducive to doing focused work than others; partly as a function of the environment (the library might be better than a bar or loud restaurant), and partly depending on what works better for you. Usually quiet places, where others are also studying, works well, like libraries and reading rooms. Sometimes a place that is too quiet and empty puts people off, or a particular library can be a place where all your friends are, and it is hard to concentrate when you want to go over and chat.

Some of you may not have the luxury of a perfectly quiet environment, or be able to go to the library to study. I don't think having less than ideal circumstances means you can't focus, it simply means you have to work slightly harder at it. I studied for my entire 10th and 12th board high school exams (O-level and A-level equivalents) without a desk, studying mostly on my bed, and at times on the dining table. The desk I had was small and was mostly taken up by my computer monitor and keyboard. As I did most of my school work by hand, I just worked wherever I found space.

With a bit of trial and error, find what works for you. The right study spot is where you can set up and immediately start to study. If it's a place you only go to get work done, as soon as you sit down, your brain will know that it's time to get serious. It could be the same floor of the library, or the same empty classroom, or even the desk in your dorm room. Unfortunately, even a great study spot can lose its luster if overused, or if you're tackling something unusually difficult.

Change Your Environment

Sometimes you start to feel stuck, you've been staring at the same wallpaper behind your desk for too long, or you're just getting restless. Just a change of environment, even something subtle, can make a huge difference. Many famous writers use this trick to get themselves back in the flow of their work. Woody Allen paces around his apartment balcony when he gets stuck on a screenplay, and the late Maya Angelou often went to a hotel room to write because she felt too distracted at home. You too can take a cue from these celebrated writers - sometimes just moving from one study spot to another can shake you out of your inertia. Research has also shown that studying in different environments can increase the amount you remember when for a test compared to always studying at the same place.

So go ahead and experiment with different places to study on campus and near your home. Maybe there is a quiet coffee shop that isn't as crowded as the library, has comfy chairs and free Wi-Fi. Maybe the local library has some hidden study spots that are good for concentrated work. Maybe you can take your books out-of-doors if the weather is nice. The trick is to do something that feels like a change, but also pick a place that helps you focus, not get further distracted.

I also always liked to pick different locations for different types of work. At my undergraduate university, a new study space was built by the school, with lots of comfortable seating as well as banks of computer terminals. I generally liked to write my papers there, preferring to be around other students to do something I found difficult. On the other hand, to learn material for an exam, I needed total isolation. I discovered empty classrooms, where I used the blackboards to lecture to myself and memorize the case law for exams. At other times, when the weather was nice, I walked to a small pond on campus, where the ducks serenely swam by, and I read my textbooks or edited printed copies of my term papers. The environment made it easy to spend a lot of time doing focused work, but at the same time, I felt relaxed watching the ripples on the water and feeling the gentle breeze on my face.

An easier option if you're constrained to one study spot is to move things around in your study space. I used to sometimes move the furniture around my bedroom if I was feeling stuck - facing the bed by the window instead of the desk, moving the lamp around, anything to press the reset button and get me out of my funk. I read somewhere that some *feng shui* experts claim that simply moving furniture around can change the energy of a room. While I can't vouch for the science behind it, I always found that it made a difference.

No one study environment is suitable for everyone all the time, and if you feel that yours isn't working for you - feel free to change it up. You might even need to keep a few favorite places in rotation - so that when one becomes stale (or gets overcrowded), you can find somewhere else.

Tip #18

You Don't Need To Be a Grind

You might think that in order to get good grades you need to be a grind - study every spare minute you can, put in hours of work, and sacrifice all fun and social activities. Maybe you decided that you don't relish the idea of being a boring person who never has time for fun, and decided that trying to go for good grades was too much trouble and therefore didn't bother to put in the work. Instead, you resigned yourself to poor grades.

Or maybe you are the student who the others make fun of, for consistently getting the highest grades. Maybe studying is all you do, not because you enjoy it all that much, but you're afraid that if you don't your grades will drop, and then you won't get into the best college or the best job. Or maybe you're just afraid that if you take time off from studying and have a little fun, you will like it too much. Maybe you think that you will become too lazy.

This was definitely me in college – although I did goof off a lot in my first year, I also believed that studying was an all-or-nothing proposition – either I had fun or I worked hard. I wasn't able to find a balance, especially during my Masters', when I turned down many more invitations than I accepted, and mostly went out only for 'official' functions, which made me unhappier and more stressed than I needed to be. It was much later that I realized taking breaks, doing a few fun things, whether alone or with friends, can actually refresh you and bring you back to your work with enthusiasm.

Doing well in school isn't necessarily about studying a lot. I think you can choose a middle path - you can study reasonable hours, while using effective strategies and tools that maximize the time you are putting in. Using the advice in this book can help you to improve your grades significantly, and still have time for some fun, by using the time you do spend studying better, and making better use of your overall time in general.

Some students may appear to be naturally gifted in certain subjects, although that is probably a result of them simply spending more time on those subjects. You may see these 'naturals' and feel dejected and worry that you won't measure up. Even if you're falling spectacularly behind, you can modify your study strategies and improve. You could also use these tactics to get an edge even if you aim for the top scores in your class or in standardized exams. The skills and mindsets presented here are flexible enough to be adapted to your specific situation.

Taking breaks and living a balanced life can actually make you more effective. Numerous books and scientific articles show the benefit of confining your work hours, including time for activities that truly relax and energize you, and making time to look after yourself, physically and emotionally. Allow yourself to indulge in a few hobbies, volunteer with a cause you care about, or take up some form of physical activity, even if it is only going for long walks. Not only will your studies not suffer, if you're strategic about it, you could actually get better at your schoolwork and become a more well-rounded person at the same time. The tools in this book are intended to help you to study reasonable hours and still get good grades. You won't be able to skate by with no or tiny amounts of work, but by matching your study strategies to how your brain works, closely monitoring how you spend your study time (removing inefficiencies and distractions) and following the principles laid out in the book, you can dramatically improve your grades while still having a life.

Chapter 5
Beating Procrastination

"Procrastination is like a credit card: it's a lot of fun until you get the bill."

– Christopher Parker.

All of us procrastinate at some point or other. It is natural to feel overwhelmed by how much we have to do, or try to escape from an activity that we aren't good at - our minds naturally want to escape to something else that feels good in the moment. However, it becomes a problem when we regularly can't seem to get started on important school work, when we miss deadlines or just scrape something together at the last minute, when we are constantly stressed about how much we need to do, or when we end up saying no to something fun because we have to work on an assignment at the last minute.

If you think that your tendency to procrastinate is so out of hand that you can't get anything done till hours before a deadline, or if you have never experienced the joy of handing in an assignment ahead of time and relaxing instead of pulling yet another all-nighter, help is at hand. This section gives some strategies to help you combat procrastination and become more productive.

Tip #19

Start With Low-Hanging Fruit

Tackle Pesky Perfectionism

Procrastination often comes from perfectionism, wanting to do something right or perfectly. You could probably write the paper you are avoiding, or work on the book report, but you're afraid you will not do a good enough job, and so you avoid it altogether. The roots of perfectionism masquerading as procrastination also stem from incorrect beliefs; for instance, that you need to do the work all in one session, or that it must be difficult otherwise you are doing it wrong. Perfectionists want to start with the most difficult aspect of a project, or otherwise insist on starting from the beginning and moving linearly until the end.

Beat procrastination by becoming pragmatic - decide that the main goal is to get the job done, initially without worrying about quality or in what order it gets done. The reason this works is that it is a great antidote to perfectionism. When just getting down to work seems hard, or your to-do list of assignments and reading seems too long, it's the easiest way to motivate yourself. Start with the easiest parts of a project or assignment first, or the easiest assignment on your list. Focus on just doing the work, even if initially you do it badly.

Start Small and Win Big

So how does this work? From the list of assignments you anyway need to do (which includes prep for upcoming tests and papers), pick the simplest task and get that done. Finishing something, even something really small and easy, can provide the motivation to keep going on the other tasks. Just starting can be the hardest part - once you've gotten going, you might find it's not as hard to keep up the momentum.

Small wins can add up - on days when motivating yourself is hard, and your concentration is flagging - it might be difficult to get into a big, complicated assignment. But you could probably do two or three of the small tasks on your list - write a short one to two-page paper, start the research for a term paper, do the reading for the most interesting course. Find whatever appeals to you, and do that. Set a timer (see section tip #21) for 20 minutes and do one task.

This trick gets you into the habit of doing work regularly, even if it's a small amount. Also by doing some easy things, you will find more easy things; often completing one aspect of a project can shed light on the other parts of the project and make them seem relatively easier. This also allows you to start working on projects or assignments earlier. Usually, procrastinators wait until the last minute to start something, which can be dangerous because often we underestimate how long something might take, and doing it in one big rush usually results in much poorer quality work. Allowing yourself to start on the simplest aspect of a project, whatever that might be, allows you to start earlier, and results in better quality work and lower stress.

Tip #20

Break Up Large Projects

Series of Smaller Tasks

The biggest source of fear and stress for me in college was writing those long papers that inevitably constituted at least 50% or more of my grade. I was never particularly good at writing papers - always getting dreadful grades on a paper I spent weeks sweating over, and surprisingly good grades over those I just banged out right before the deadline. Seeing that a class had a significant portion of the grade assigned to a research paper always made me frantic. One main reason for this fear was that I saw the paper as one large task, and its enormity scared me.

Since I started to work on projects spanning months, working with other people and multiple deadlines, I have learned to break big projects down into more manageable chunks. All large projects are basically a series of related tasks; some tasks are smaller, while others may take a couple of work sessions. Even when you don't know exactly how many steps or stages are involved, you can guess, and usually the first few steps are quite apparent.

When you are first assigned a large task - a paper that is 20 - 30 pages long, or a presentation or project - write down, in no particular order, all the steps (based on what you know now) that you think you will need to go through. For instance, you may need to find a topic, do some preliminary research, get approval from your Professor, create the slides for the presentation, and so on. Once you have a list of everything you can think of, put the steps in an order that seems logical - for instance you would need to do research and finalize a topic before you can write a draft. Based on the final submission deadline - estimate how much time you have to complete each step.

If you're not sure how to break your project down into smaller steps, try Googling it - steps to write a thesis, for instance. You could also ask others who have done similar projects before. Don't spend too much time on this step – the idea is that you break one big project with one looming deadline, into smaller, more manageable portions. How you break that up is less important.

Set Mini-Deadlines

The reason most of us procrastinate for weeks or months on a large project, and the panic towards the final deadline, is that we have only one large deadline to work towards. Instead, create mini-deadlines for each major phase of your project. For instance, set a deadline for completing research, another deadline for a rough draft, and a final deadline, a few days before the actual submission date, for the completion of the final draft. Some Professors actually give smaller deadlines to ensure that students do the work on a regular time table - assigning a proposal or some short first steps that are required and graded separately from the final submission. Even when you only have one final submission date, you can always use your mini-deadlines to get feedback at each stage from your instructor, to ensure that your work is progressing well and that you are on the right track.

Once you have broken the task list down and assigned mini-deadlines, add these to your calendar, with appropriate reminders. Also remember to add each step to your weekly plan the week you plan to get it done. If a step will take more than a week, maybe you can break it down even further.

One advantage of advance planning is that it allows you to create a buffer - in case any step takes longer than you imagined, or some other unseen problems come up. If you have extra time, you could use it to incorporate feedback from your Professor, or get help from your school's writing center if you have one. They might be able to help you improve the structure of your arguments, or point out sections that are a bit weaker, giving you time to improve it. If you don't have the benefit of a writing center - you could ask a friend who writes good papers to take a look at it. For projects that are a big portion of your grade, giving yourself enough time to plan, do the work and get feedback, could help you to really improve your grade.

With this method, even the largest project is doable. And if you plan early enough – you can squeeze a large project into an already busy life – just by tackling it in small steps.

Tip #21

Use a Timer

Sometimes it feels like you just can't bear to start working, you have mountains of work, piles of reading, tons of assignments, and it all feels so overwhelming you would rather not get started at all. Even when you have a plan, it can seem like there is so much to do, you don't even know where to start. Starting something can be the hardest part – you see how much there is to do and balk. Even when you have followed the advice in the previous section and broken a task down, it is still difficult sometimes to get going on the first task. It is easy to say to yourself – "oh I have to work for the next four hours straight, so why not just grab a quick snack? And make a phone call before I start - then I will definitely get down to work." This sort of procrastination can, unfortunately, go on for a while. (In fact, I did just that while working on this book!)

The way to break this cycle and get some momentum on the work you need to get done is to use a timer. The method is simple - set a timer for a set number of minutes, switch off your phone, and start work on a task, and keep at it till the timer goes off. You can use an old-fashioned timer (a real one that you wind up) or one on your phone or computer.

This technique is advocated by many writing teachers, as it helps to break past the block and get started, often the hardest part. Productivity books extol the Pomodoro technique - which involves setting a timer for 25 minutes, working on the first task, then taking a 5 minute break, and setting the timer again for the 2nd task, then taking another 5 minute break. After four rounds, you can take a longer break, such as for 30 minutes. This is called the Pomodoro method because the inventor of this method used a timer shaped like a *pomodoro* (or tomato in Italian).

I would suggest choosing a time length based on what your

task is, and how difficult you're finding getting going. If you need to start your math or economics homework, you may need at least 25 minutes to get going. On the other hand, maybe you're finding that the idea of starting work on your history reading or writing the first draft of your political science paper due in a few days is too daunting; in that case, set the timer initially just for 15 minutes. You can always psych yourself up to work for 15 minutes, and it might be just the thing to get over your hump - and you might find yourself working even after the timer goes off.

I usually find just one or two timed sessions are enough to get me going - but feel free to use this technique as many times as you need it during your work session. Many professionals use timers to get their tasks done at work - it can actually be an incredibly useful technique just to overcome the initial inertia to get started.

Tip #22

Use Bribes and Incentives

Animal trainers know this instinctively – give the animal treats and praise for doing something right, and they will learn faster and more enthusiastically. Punish them, and they may still learn, but they will be sad and beaten down. Unfortunately, our human schools and educational systems don't seem to have got the message. When we do something right, it's hard to get anything more enthusiastic than a throwaway or distracted "that's nice". When things don't go well on the other hand, no one is shy about speaking up. I don't remember getting too much praise from the extended members of my family as a child, but I vividly remember all the criticism, which despite myself, I slowly internalized and they turned into voices in my head, telling me why I couldn't do certain things. There are cultural forces at work here of course, and certain communities lean more towards praise and others towards criticism; however, I think across the breadth of all academic and extra-curricular activities, it is more common to encounter environments where the focus is on the negative.

Many of us have deep-rooted bad habits and blocks that prevent us from learning to our potential or cause us to believe that we can't improve, and we fail to even try. One of the ways to inculcate better study habits (or any habit really), is to do something regularly and then reward ourselves for doing it. The reward acts as a signal to our brain that tells us that this activity is good, and we must repeat it in the future. This method is in sharp contrast with the way that many of us have tried to instill new habits in the past; we decide to make a change, fail a few times, criticize ourselves harshly and then decide that we are just not capable of change.

Our old habits and routines are difficult to change for the

same reason that we don't forget how to multiply after we have learned to do it automatically. The routine is embedded in our mind, and is difficult to erase. The only way to change is by creating a new habit or routine that becomes equally embedded. Habits can be our friend, so that actions that are difficult for us to do now, like start our homework early, spend more time tackling difficult subjects, planning our work, become easier and more automatic.

One way to do this is to pick an action that we want to make a habit, such as creating a daily plan, and then build a routine around it. In the book *The Power of Habit*, author Charles Duhigg explains that habits are composed of three elements – a cue, an action, and a reward or payoff. He gives the example that every day around 4 pm, he would go to the cafeteria and get a cookie and eat it. In this case, 4 pm is the cue, and the action is eating the cookie. The reward he realized was that around that time he started to lose energy and crave some company, so walking to the cafeteria, and eating the cookie while chatting to co-workers, provided an energy boost and some camaraderie. He then explained how he changed this cookie habit over time, by substituting the reward from the cookie with something else.

You can similarly use rewards as a way to change your behavior. The objective is to tie proportional rewards with actions that you want to do. Let's say you need to write a large paper. You could break the paper into stages: research, create an outline, write a draft, and then revise and polish the paper. You could give yourself mini-treats after the completion of each stage, such as going to watch a movie or eating lunch at your favorite restaurant. You obviously can't do this for every assignment or paper, but you could use this strategy for difficult assignments or ones that account for a large part of your grade and you find yourself putting off working on them.

Modify the system and create mini-rewards of things you like to do more regularly and tie them to getting your work done.

Maybe there is a TV show that you absolutely must watch each week. Could you tackle your weekly math homework and then watch the show as a reward? Or maybe you can complete your history reading before joining your friends to play football. That way, not only will you enjoy the activity you like to do, but you can do it knowing that you got something difficult accomplished beforehand.

A technique I use when I have a lot of work to do for certain projects that have a fast approaching deadline, or the work is particularly difficult, is to resort to kindergarten tricks. I buy pages of colored stickers – the ones you get in the stationery section of stores, in uniform shapes and colors. I break my work down into tasks that are similar – for instance, I need to type up 60 pages of a manuscript I wrote by hand, or I need to write 20 sections for a report. On a fresh sheet of paper, I label the task, and then as I complete each section (or type each page or whatever), I add a sticker on the page. It may be slightly juvenile, but it can be really fun to see the stickers add up. Sometimes I use different colored stickers for each day, so I can see at a glance that yesterday, for instance, I completed six sections, and then try to set up a competition with myself, so that I can get more stickers today than I did the day before. Dr. Naoisé O'Reilly, an educationalist who works with students with learning difficulties, and herself suffers from dyslexia, enthusiastically recommends such unorthodox methods, both for children and adults. "The goal should be achievable and have the right level of challenge, so there's a balance there. At one stage, when I was finding school very hard because of my dyslexia, my parents set up a reward system. It was achievable, but I had to work hard. If I did well in a project at school, I would collect rewards. They were kind of like Green Shield stamps... It gave me a massive sense of achievement..."

The system of rewards for tasks uses the same principle used by video games – the pleasure centers of our brain lights up when we get rewards, even if they are meaningless ones like stickers or virtual XP or battle swords. Even though we consciously know that the rewards are just tokens, subconsciously we are still motivated by wanting them. Why not harness this human quirk and "gamify" your schoolwork?

Tip #23

Harness Productive Procrastination

Sometimes even though you have tried all the tricks, nothing seems to be working, and you just can't make progress on an important task. Or you know you need to study, but since you don't really want to work on the most important assignment you have, you procrastinate and watch some TV or play some video games instead. When I feel like this, I resort to productive procrastination!

What do I mean by "productive procrastination"? Isn't that an oxymoron (a combination of words that have opposite or very different meanings)? Well we all procrastinate, even though we know it's a waste of time, causes stress, and we know we shouldn't be doing it. Some of us are even worse procrastinators than others (I'm definitely raising my hand here - in fact, I put off working on this section!), finding it difficult to get things done on a regular basis, and waiting until the last minute and scrambling. It's never really a good feeling.

Well, this tactic acknowledges your tendency to procrastinate, and urges you to give into it rather than fighting it. Yes, you read that correctly. I first read about this idea in an essay by Professor John Perry, and realized that not only was it a powerful idea, but also that I had already been using it myself over the years, without realizing it and making full use of the notion.

Professor John Perry calls this "structured procrastination", but I prefer to term it more accurately "productive procrastination". Perry describes his method in this way: when you have a long to-do list and you have several items you must do, procrastinate on one must-do item by working on something else. While you're putting off something you need to do, you can simply do something else you need to do that doesn't seem so difficult in comparison. He suggests putting something non-urgent at the top of your list as the item to procrastinate, such as learning a language, and then using that as the incentive to get things done.

I found the idea compelling; however, Professor Perry's approach of putting obviously non-urgent items on the list doesn't work for me, because I know that there are other more important priorities. Whenever I have something important to do, I feel the urge to put it off. The way it works for me then is to change what is that day the most important priority, which helps me to get other things done. The way the procrastination then becomes "productive" is to substitute a useful task in place of simply watching TV or playing Candy Crush. So if I have writing to do, often I will get dreaded piles of laundry done, or my room dusted. Or go for a walk. Or even work on something else I was putting off earlier, because now magically it seems more appealing than what I'm avoiding. The trick here is to find important things to put off that won't cause too many problems if you put off for a while, and yet is difficult enough that you genuinely want to avoid it. One of my favorite things to procrastinate over is going to the gym or writing blog posts. As long as they are more urgent in my mind than writing (because I know that they can't be put off indefinitely), I actually get a lot of writing done.

Although this trick does seem strange and may not work for everyone, as long as you don't miss any deadlines, I suggest giving it a try. Next time you can't face your math homework, tackle that book you've been avoiding starting to read for your literature class, it will suddenly seem less odious now compared to calculus problems. Or put off cleaning your room by organizing your notes for an upcoming exam. You'll be productive, and be working with, rather than against, your real nature!

I used this technique to study for exams throughout high school. Some days switching from one subject to another did the trick, other days I was so restless, I kept switching. Not ideal, but still better than simply goofing off. And I did get something done. The less urgent whatever you're putting off doing is, the better (and safer) results you will have with this technique.

If absolutely at a loss, use the time to do study-related tasks that sometimes fall by the wayside - like clearing your desk, or filing your many pieces of paper subject-wise (see tip #13). You can spend the time searching for practice problems or start researching your paper topics online. These are tasks that need to get done, and doing them now rather than later when it might take up valuable study time, actually makes you quite productive!

The desire to put things off, to do what we *feel* like doing rather than what we *ought* to do grips everyone, but I have found that what separates productive and successful students from others is that they have a bunch of tricks up their sleeve that they pull out when they don't feel motivated and work still needs to get done. Borrow a few of these tricks, and see the difference in your own productivity.

Chapter 6
Studying Effectively

"Success is the sum of small efforts, repeated day in and day out."

— Robert Collier

Most of us think that we know the right way to study - after all we have been in school for most of our lives! Unfortunately, though our technology is state-of-the-art, the knowledge most of us have of our most important tool, our brain, is almost primitive. We perpetuate the same study habits over decades, regardless of whether we are in Manchester or Mumbai - we try to cram the information we need to know, waiting till the last possible moment, then staying up late to learn a semester's worth of information in one long, caffeine-fueled session. We read textbooks by using up a small store's worth of stationery - highlighting in bright colors and liberally applying Post-it® notes. We focus more on the subjects that come easier to us, while procrastinating and leaving for the last minute studying for classes that we struggle with.

This section tackles the actual strategies of studying day to day. You will learn about the limitations and quirks of your brain, and how best to use this knowledge to improve your study habits. You will also learn how to harness your own unique learning style, study actively and get your assignments done painlessly.

Tip #24

Leverage The Power Of Your Brain

By leveraging how your brain works, your study sessions will be more productive, and you will learn more and remember more. So far this book has explored how to plan and organize your work, study in a focused way without distractions, and how to overcome the desire to procrastinate. This chapter will explore the nuts and bolts of studying - how to best use the time when you do sit down to work, what exactly should you be doing, and why.

Working Memory: The Need For Focus

Our brains are pretty amazing – we can do many things that computers are only recently being trained to do – such as recognize faces, and detect patterns in games of skill such as chess. Highly-skilled human beings are able to outperform computers in many areas. This is possible because our brains have been designed to learn, to make new connections, and to master skills that are important to us. At the same time, every day we process millions of pieces of information, most of them without even consciously registering that we are doing so. Just a simple task such as grocery shopping, involves hundreds of thousands of cognitive processes -- we take in information about what is available, we think about what we want to buy, we look at the other people also shopping, perhaps recognizing a friend, and we do all this with an awareness that we need to be efficient and finish by a certain time. Our mind allows many pieces of information to fly by us, because if we stopped to consciously register everything, our brain (well the conscious part) would be quickly overwhelmed and even the smallest task would become impossible. Thus, we only register those things that we have already "primed" our mind to focus on – for example, by making a grocery list.

This, unfortunately, hampers us when we are studying. If we casually read, or try to study while doing other things, like watching TV, the information we are learning just washes over us and doesn't really register in our mind. In order to remember things, we have to signal to our brain that something is important. Research has shown that in order to form a long-term memory, we need to pay close attention to that information. We have to create a neural pathway, and reinforce those pathways in our mind, so that we can return to them again later when we need to. This is done by consciously processing the information, as well as recalling it enough times to embed it in our long-term memory.

As we saw in chapter 3, we have limited space in our working memory, the part of our brain's short-term memory that consciously processes items of information. Therefore we cannot juggle too many pieces of information, or work on many things at once. If we add something, like trying to remember "Call Sam" or "Pick up library book", something else tends to fall off. Trying to do different kinds of thinking, such as trying to remember points and organize them at the same time, can be too much for our brain because it overloads the working memory.

One way to increase how much we can process at one time, and become better at what we are learning, is to link in our minds things that go together, almost like sausages in a chain, so that more items can fit in less slots in our working memory. We can do this by *chunking* the information we take in.

Chunking: Break It Down and Build It Up

You know the feeling you get when you're watching an incredible performance – of a dancer, musician or athlete? You look at them and wonder how they have such amazing proficiency and grace? They built it up through a process called *chunking*.

Chunking basically means to take an aspect of a skill, and then internalize it in such a way that it becomes effortless. Those who are experts at any skill – whether chess or golf or calculus – have basically broken their subject down into chunks, mastered those chunks, then put them together in larger pieces. Chunking allows you to work with a lot of different pieces of information, without overwhelming your limited working memory. Once you master certain concepts and skills, those concepts take up less space in your working memory, leaving you room to learn something else.

Let's look at it another way. If you have ever attended a dance or group fitness class, there is usually a routine that is taught during the class. The instructor may start by demonstrating the whole routine, which could look incredibly complicated. Then they start to show you how to do it. You step to the right and then to the left. You clap your hands and turn. You practice that a few times, then you add one more step. Then you put those three steps together and practice it, this time a little faster. Then the instructor shows you three more steps. Then you practice the whole thing from the beginning. Soon you start to execute an entire mini-dance sequence – all of which you learned simply by *chunking* it – breaking it down into smaller component parts, mastering those parts, and then putting them together.

You can use this method to learn your school material as well. Your syllabus and textbooks already break your topics into sections. Break those down further – taking each concrete piece or problem as a chunk – and then break it down further until you have mastered the smallest steps or learned the simplest facts. Then put the pieces together, and form a chunk. Learn that chunk, practice it, internalize it. As you keep doing this for your material, you will start to form larger and larger chunks. In math, solving a quadratic equation can be a chunk. Then solving a word problem involving quadratic equations can be a second chunk – first turning the word problem into an equation, and then solving the equation. The whole thing is now an even larger chunk. Eventually, you will have chunked algebra, or geometry – at least for your grade level. Then no matter what problem you are given, you can solve it. If you have friends who are able to solve any sum effortlessly, it might seem like they are just born with that talent, but trust me, it's simply a function of chunking. No one is born knowing how to solve for x; they might have had more practice, or they might intuitively understand some of the steps that you might need to take more time to internalize. The same principles guide how everyone learns, although people master phases or steps at different paces.

Practicing Deliberately

Deliberate practice (or *deep practice* as it is sometimes called) is a particular method of practicing something so as to internalize it and build expertise. We have all been told to practice till we get better. Turns out that actually works really well, and especially well if its deliberate practice. What does it mean? Deliberate practice is a way to supercharge your learning, so that you build more connections in your mind, strengthening that pathway I mentioned earlier. The stronger the pathways or *neural circuits* in our mind, the faster and more accurately our brain can send the signal to recall an important fact or solve a particular problem when we need to.

Research in the last few years has shown that every skill, every complex physical or mental action performed by us, is not just a function of neurons that send signals from one part of the brain to another, but also a function of how much white matter or *myelin* is sheathed or wrapped around the axon (or branch) of our neurons. Myelin is now thought to govern the accuracy and speed of our skills, and research shows that the more we practice *in a certain way*, the more myelin we create for that skill and the better we get at it. If you just started to learn to ride a bike for instance, you don't have much skill at it yet – perhaps you fall down a lot. But the more you practice, (and thereby the more myelin you generate around riding a bike), the better you get at it, eventually flying down the path with your friends.

How do you develop a skill, any skill? Short answer – develop more myelin. How do you do that? Practice the skill repeatedly, fixing any errors and getting feedback on the correct way to do it. This specific kind of practice is termed *deliberate* or *deep practice*. This concept was first defined by noted psychologist Dr. K. Anders Ericsson, who claimed that most so-called "geniuses" aren't born that way, but became stars of their field through building expertise over a period of time, specifically by practicing in a way that was very different from how the less successful people practiced. He demonstrated his theories in experiments with musicians, chess players and sportspersons.

Ok, so how does it apply to studying? The hallmark of *deliberate practice* is that it requires you to be as actively engaged as possible, rooting out errors and getting feedback so that you can improve your performance. It requires more from you while you're doing it. You need to be alert, you need to work on something that is new or difficult, something that you struggle with, as opposed to something you already know how to do easily. "It entails considerable, specific, and sustained efforts to do something you can't do well—or even at all. Research across domains shows that it is only by working at what you can't do that you turn into the expert you want to become." Most people opt to do what comes easily to them – whether they are beginners or experts. Champion golfer Sam Snead said, "It is only human nature to want to practice what you can already do well, since it's a hell of a lot less work and a hell of a lot more fun". That's why deliberate practice is so effective in separating those who are at the top of their fields from everyone else – because it is difficult to do, and thus it is not often done.

Since this book is about improving your grades without

sacrificing your other activities or increasing your stress levels, deliberate practice is one of the most potent tools for you to learn new material and do well in assessments. Maybe you're trying to internalize a new topic in physics that you just learned in school. You decide to practice the concept from a supplementary book which has worked-out sample problems in it. You copy the first problem into your notebook, and then try to solve it on your own. It's hard, but you remember the formulae to use, and you apply it. Then you check your answer with that in the book. You got it wrong, because you made an error in converting the units. You try the next problem, again working on it yourself, and then checking to see if it was the right answer.

Working on something new feels like an intense mental struggle because you will be trying really hard to figure out how to solve the problem or understand the concept. That's why this technique is powerful, because you're operating outside your comfort zone, and struggling to master something that is just out of your reach. You can usually also get almost instant feedback – you solve the problem and then look up the answer, or test yourself on the facts and see which ones you got wrong. This tells you where you went wrong and how to fix it. In tip #30 I discuss using supplementary materials, one of the main reasons is to have more sources for deliberate practice. The more you push yourself and struggle to learn the material, the faster you will learn it, and be able to apply it when tested.

One way to understand this, is to think about driving. When we learn to drive, we have to remember a lot of different instructions - wear a seat belt, press the accelerator, slide into first gear, keep foot close to brake, look in your mirrors. As we learn all this, we are creating patterns in our mind and activating mental maps associated with driving. At first we have to think consciously about all those things, and we might panic if unexpectedly a car swerves at us or honks impatiently. As we keep practicing, we build up enough skill so that a lot of the processes and steps become automatic. Soon we don't even have to think about it, and can carry on a conversation and parallel park at the same time.

What deliberate practice does therefore is it makes skills we are trying to learn automatic or embedded in our neural patterns. When we try to learn something, make a mistake, and then correct that mistake, it reinforces the pattern for that ability in our mind. Over time the ability becomes automatic and we no longer need to think about it.

That's really the secret to improving at your studies and getting better grades fast, without spending all of your time studying. Most students spend their time studying either on re-reading the material, or focusing on subjects they find easy. The way to get good at a particular subject is to systematically identify your weaknesses, find the way to do it correctly, get feedback, and start the loop again. For instance, if you're having trouble in math, and you consistently get all sums involving calculus wrong, you need to spend most of your math study time, at least initially, on calculus problems. Try practice ones from the book, then compare your answer and see where you're going wrong. Focusing on doing sample problems on your own and then checking the answers gives you a chance to build the skill, to figure it out for yourself, and then get almost instant feedback. Those two in conjunction are very important.

Spending even a small amount of time on your weaknesses can dramatically improve your grades. It can be really frustrating to work on your weaknesses - you're mentally struggling, stretching. It is awkward, uncomfortable. But this is also the sign that you're growing, that you're on the right track. The longer you are able to endure this feeling of awkwardness, the more progress you will make. Because this is mentally very exhausting, you need to approach such work fresh, get enough sleep, and tackle it in short bursts.

Space Out Your Learning

Spreading out your studying, and doing short focused stints of work on a topic, and then coming back again later to it is better than trying to power through or pulling an all-nighter, to get something done. Rather than trying to study eight hours on the Sunday before an exam, you are better off putting in four 2-hour sessions - it is far less painful, and you will see the dramatic difference in your grades, as well as how much you remember weeks after the exam.

Studies have shown that breaking up your learning over a period of time is a much better strategy than learning everything in one long session - essentially cramming. When we cram all our learning into one session, probably the day or night before the exam, we may remember just enough for the test, but we don't remember anything weeks or months later. Since you aren't studying just to pass one test, but hopefully in order to use the learning later, (even if you don't plan to use the learning, many courses build upon each other, and by not remembering the material from earlier semesters, you can find things even harder), cramming to get through assessments essentially wastes your time because you don't remember anything and may have to learn it again.

Research shows that performance on tests is improved if multiple study sessions are "spaced" apart in time. The researchers found that studying information across two or more sessions that are spread apart (on different days) was far more effective in terms of learning than if the students spent the same amount of time studying the material in one session. The final performance on the test for those who spread the studying out was better than for those who did it all in one session; this phenomenon is referred to as the *spacing effect*. The research doesn't, however, show consistent data on how many days' gap is optimal for the best results – it depends on when you will be tested on the material. For tests that are further away, studying in longer gaps gives a better result, whereas for tests that are only a few days away, studying every day for shorter periods is more effective.

The way to imprint things in your mind so that you can remember them for a longer time, and to study much more painlessly than you are probably used to is a simple but very effective strategy - break up your study sessions on a topic. Study the topic soon after you learn it, then a few days later, and a few days after that, giving your brain ample time to process and store the material properly. This sort of spaced repetition can seem very different from the kind of studying you are used to - long sessions trying to memorize something, usually long after you first learn it - and is actually far more effective. Spaced repetition is also effective because it invokes the diffuse mode of your brain. For instance, you work on your assignments or try to learn something new in focused mode, then you take a break. During this time your brain is processing this new information in the background without you being consciously aware of it, and when you get back to looking at your work in a focused manner, you may already have some insights and new understanding.

The study techniques in this book utilize this concept of spaced repetition in several ways. When preparing for tests that require you to learn information like dates or definitions, just create flashcards (either physical or digital) with the material you need to learn, and then set aside small chunks of time to learn them -- you can even do this while on the treadmill or waiting in line or traveling by public transport, if you make the cards and carry them or have an app on your phone. Certain apps also have built-in algorithms that repeat those concepts or words you're struggling with more frequently.

When doing assignments for school, set aside several short sessions of one to two hours each, to tackle your assignments (see tip #27 for more details). Start homework assignments as soon as possible, and work on them in short focused sessions. Instead of trying to learn all the techniques of a topic or do all the questions on one day, by spreading out the work you allow your brain to consolidate the material and understand it better by making connections with existing knowledge.

By spreading your work out over time, you are also able to come at with renewed energy and focus. Cal Newport, the author of several books on study skills and a popular blogger, demonstrated why this is such a powerful technique using a simple example. Let's say you spend four hours studying on Sunday, the day before your test. The first hour you study with an intensity of 10, the next hour 8, the next hour - by which time you're already quite tired - your intensity drops to 4, and the final hour, let's say it is 1 (you're really distracted and finding it hard to focus now). So your total intensity is 23. Instead, if you study for 3 sessions - one hour each of 10 intensity, and one two-hour slot of 10 + 8 intensity – which gives you a total of 38. That's a big difference, in the quality and amount of work you get done, and can make a lot of difference in the quality of your grade as well.

Therefore the best way to benefit from the *spacing effect* is to start revision of the material as early after first learning it as possible. If you're learning for a history test for instance, you can create flashcards, or notes in a Q&A format within days of learning the material in class. Then, depending on when your test is, you can revise the material at least two or three times before the test, at regular intervals. In this way, when conducting your final review session a few days before the test, you will simply need to refresh your memory, not learn something for the first time.

Interleaving Your Study Sessions

Interleaving is a study technique related to spaced repetition that is also very effective. Studies have shown that when you spend time learning one thing, and then take a break and move on to something else – this enables you to learn more rather than doing the same thing at a stretch for hours. Research on students who studied different topics within the same subject, versus those who focused on only one topic, showed that the students who *interleaved* their studying performed significantly better on the test (by more than 40%). Imagine an athlete training for the gymnastics – they move around between the beam, bars and floor routine – doing different things through the day, working different muscle groups. When we do the same thing for hours, our brain gets fatigued and stops working in peak capacity. Changing around and working on different subjects can actually give the brain a break, and allows it to focus more intently on the new topic. In the meantime, our mind is still working away in diffuse mode on the previous topic, so when we come back to the old subject, we can make unexpected progress. This is also an effective technique for studying subjects like mathematics or economics, where interleaving the problems you practice can improve your learning not only of how to solve the problems but also in knowing what techniques to apply in which types of problems.

Now that we have reviewed some insights from the latest research into how we learn, let's look at how to incorporate that into your daily study routine.

Tip #25

Learn Actively

Avoid Passive Reading

The best way to learn material we will be tested on is being engaged with the topic and learning actively. This is unfortunately not the way most students approach studying -- we highlight our textbook or reading material, thinking we read it so now we understand and know it. That's misleading – and many of us find that out the hard way, after doing badly in a test even though "we studied". Passive reading and highlighting are ineffective study methods, because the material "washes over us like a warm bath" and doesn't really register in our minds.

As the previous section illustrated, the material you are studying will only get embedded in your mind if you struggle to grasp it. By engaging with the material, and taking notes that analyze the information, rather than simply copying mindlessly, you will "fire your neural circuits", and strengthen the connections made by the material in your mind, so that the next time you need it, you will be able to access the information more easily. When you passively read or highlight, however, while it seems that you may be getting more familiar with the material, when later you are tested, you may not remember most of what you read. This is because instead of doing the hard work of sorting and organizing or even summarizing the main points, you relied on simply remembering it automatically.

In order to make the most of your study time, you need to leave behind any study habits that are ineffective. Most top students (and books on study skills) agree that passive reading is usually a complete waste of time. Instead, spend your time actively engaged with the material, internalizing and being able to apply it. This starts with what you do in class.

Taking Notes in Class

While most study advice books focus a lot on the best way to take notes in class, with each one teaching or advocating for a specific method, I don't have any rigid rules about note-taking. I have tried many options, such as the Cornell note-taking method, mind-mapping, and other methods. I usually just return to the straight-forward method of writing down the most important points I can, in the order it is presented. However, I do try to modify my note-taking style for each class, depending on the type of course and the instructor.

Firstly, it is important to actually attend lectures, even if the class meets at an inconvenient time, or the Professor is really boring. Being in class helps you to know what is discussed, get a good overview of the material, and get a chance to ask questions or learn from the answers to others' queries. Panagiotis, a former honors student says, "The most important thing to do is to pay attention in class. I was almost never distracted from this goal. This way I already knew about the subject after the class was over. This cut my home study more than half".

For reading intensive courses such as history, law, and political science, typing your class notes on a laptop could give you an advantage if you type faster than you write. These lectures usually have a lot of material covered in class, and being able to capture as much as possible is an advantage. If you're not sure whether your notes are complete, you could also ask your classmates for help. Dr. Margaret Reese, a student mentor, says, "A really good strategy is to compare notes with your classmates. It not only feels less lonely [than studying alone], it will tell you whether your notes are capturing the right stuff."

It is also important when taking notes to pay attention to context - some things are more important than others. For instance, when discussing an upcoming exam, your Professor may give a hint of what topics are more important to focus on; highlight, bold or draw focus in some way to this in your notes. When the Professor gives their opinions of a particular author's viewpoint, or analyses the causes for something, this is also important to highlight in your notes. If they are simply repeating facts already available in your reading, this is less important to take down. Similarly, some instructors like to post their slides on the course website or make handouts available, either before or after the lecture. In that case, you don't need to copy information that is already available, and can focus on listening to any additional commentary as well as really understanding the lecture. However, just because notes are available, don't assume that you don't need to take any notes at all; instead use this opportunity to write down a high-level summary, noting only the most crucial points, or otherwise process the information so that you have to spend less time studying afterwards, and also have something to refer to refresh your memory.

When taking notes, write down and highlight any insights or conclusions that you have drawn from the material. For instance, if an example the lecturer mentions reminds me of something else I have studied, in this class or elsewhere, I will make a note of that as I go, indicating that it's my own thought and not the lecturer's. This is something you can do in whatever way suits you – I have my own personal notation and shortcuts that I use when I'm taking notes by hand. If I am typing, I might change the font color for that point and then change back. As long as you are consistent, so that you always know what your lecturer said is different from your own thoughts. Writing down your own insights helps you to understand and retain the topics better, as well as provides valuable analysis that you can use in your assessments to illustrate your grasp of the material you've studied.

The simple act of taking notes can help imprint the information you are reading or hearing into your mind. Recent graduate Rob Mayzes says that while "everyone has their own best way of learning...[f]or me, taking notes makes a huge difference, even if I never read back those notes. Even when I'm reading a long book, I will still jot down notes to help me remember key facts. If I really need to learn something, I compile those notes into several condensed 'best of' pages to go over before an exam. Re-writing and condensing notes a second time really drills it in!" You can also summarize points, or put them into an ordered list if you have time (make sure you don't miss important points). Research shows that anything that organizes the information, whether by taking notes or creating a summary, helps you remember it longer.

When you sit down to study the material yourself, make sure to use every organizational method that occurs to you or is helpful. You could create maps, timelines, or organize your notes by idea or argument. Putting the information in some sort of order actually helps your mind retain it more easily.

Author Cal Newport suggests that instead of writing down everything the lecturer says as is, you should focus on taking down the main idea or question(s) posed by the topic, the conclusion presented by the lecturer, and the evidence relating the conclusion to the question. This method essentially forces you to process all the information of the topic into ideas, rather than free-floating facts that you then need to somehow attach to ideas. Many Professors naturally present their lecture in this format, which makes it easy to implement this method. While I commend this approach, if the lecturer doesn't explicitly follow this format, or just presents a lot of information that isn't neatly categorized into topics, typing to fit this format might be difficult during the lecture itself while the information is flying at you at top speed. It is better to spend a few minutes after the lecture, going over your notes and highlighting what evidence corresponds to what questions, or formatting the notes according to this layout. It may seem a bit of extra work, but would save a lot of time in exam preparation. My general rule is by doing extra thinking now, you save valuable time later, and gain in your grades. Where possible, however, it is best to organize and process your notes in class as much as possible, to maximize the learning opportunity, rather than simply transcribing everything the lecturer says and relying on spending more time later consciously deciding what is important and how it relates to the other topics in the course.

Taking Notes on Your Reading

Most humanities and some social sciences courses require you to read scores of journal articles, and be able to analyze and parse their arguments in seminars and term papers. At the very least, you will need to know the primary argument made in each paper by the author(s), and the evidence (at least the major pieces) that they rely on to make their point. After reading 30 - 40 pages, you may think that you know what the paper is about; after all, you meticulously went through and highlighted all the important points. The thing is, if you don't take any notes, you are unlikely to remember many details in a couple of days, and will have to skim through the paper again to remind yourself of all the main points. This wastes valuable study time, and since one of the goals of this book is to help you get better grades without chaining you to your desk, practices that save time is obviously very important.

On the other hand, you may be tempted to take detailed notes on the paper - going through each page for relevant information. This is also a waste of time, as it will take too long and you still won't be able to remember the major ideas.

The ideal is to create a short summary for each paper or book chapter. Note the author, the name of the paper and any other citation information. Then write down the main point(s) the author is making through the paper, or the main ideas discussed, and the central pieces of evidence presented. The main thesis is usually stated in the introduction to the paper and in the conclusion. Academics, unlike fiction and popular non-fiction writers, don't bury the final conclusion at the end, they usually state it up front. Start with the introduction, and then skip to the conclusion and the section on analysis and recommendations, if any. These should give you a good idea of the main argument and evidence. Then skim through the rest of the paper, noting any critical additional points, including the methodology and research method (if any). This can often be illuminating, if for instance the sample size was too small, or the methodology flawed in some other way, you could question whether the argument is really valid or widely applicable.

For book chapters or other reading which may have many complex points or ideas presented, along with a lot of evidence, you might need to vary your method slightly. Read the article or chapter straight through, making a note of the main ideas or arguments presented, numbering or ordering them in some way. Once you have read the whole piece, go back and select a few pieces of evidence to back up each argument on your list to include in your summary.

Once you have gotten the gist of the article or chapter, write down in your summary the main points, primary evidence, and any critiques that come to your mind. Make sure you note your own thoughts separately. This summary will be very useful in seminars when discussing the articles with your TAs and classmates, as well as preparing for your exam. It is also a very good starting point for research for paper topics. Be sure to note down any additional important points about the article mentioned by the Professor or TA - these can be additional critiques or further parsing of the author's arguments that could be helpful later. Doing these summaries before class will, therefore, be quite useful - and something you should keep in mind while doing your weekly plan (see tip #11).

You can also incorporate this strategy by modifying it slightly for writing papers. If you come across a paper that you know you will need for your paper topic, create a summary of that article, first making sure that you save all citation information to find it easily later. Write down the main argument and points of evidence, and also why you think it supports or detracts from the thesis of your paper, where you think you can use it, and even include any relevant quotes that you think might be useful. This extra work while you're thinking of how it fits can save you hassle later when faced with the huge task of writing your paper. You may think you will remember where each piece of research fits, but in all likelihood you won't. Having your thoughts on the page, conveniently waiting for you to use it when needed, can save hassle, time and stress, and provide a jumping off point for when you need to start writing.

Studying and Taking Notes in Technical Subjects

For technical classes, note-taking is actually quite straightforward. Make sure you take down as many examples as you can, including the steps and the final answer. If pressed for time, because the teacher is going faster than you can write everything, ensure that you at least note the answers, and any important formulae used.

For quantitative courses, where the lecturer provides lots of examples in class, draws graphs and diagrams, or there are many complicated equations, I think taking notes on paper is the best option unless you are really skilled at drawing diagrams using your word processor or using the special characters to denote equations. One exception to this is if you're using a tablet (or its equivalent) and a stylus, and essentially "writing" directly on your screen. In that case, it's not very different from using analog tools, if you're comfortable enough writing fast with them.

If you are taking notes from the textbook, focus on writing down the formulae and worked-out practice problems. If possible, highlight the formulae in your notes, or write them in another color, or even create a separate sheet with formulae. Spending time writing down worked-out versions of each type of problem, especially if you try the problem without looking at the book, is a great way to practice, because if you get stuck, you have the steps worked out to guide you. This is a perfect example of *deliberate practice.* Try practicing problems on your own, if possible working on problems that are slightly harder, just out of range. If you can effortlessly do that type of problem, skip all similar problems (except for school homework obviously) and try ones that are just one shade harder.

This is where most students give up – they expect that working through the problems, or doing the reading, should be effortless. When they start to struggle, they give up and put the work aside. Struggling in school isn't a sign that you're not smart, just that you haven't learned something *yet*. Most of us aren't born knowing how to differentiate, we all have to start somewhere and work our way up – you start with easy algebra, and then tackle harder and harder problems, till you can handle the easy problems in calculus, and then the hard ones. It's like levelling up in a video game. When you're struggling – that's when you're learning best – and if that's how you routinely approach your studying – a slightly harder problem at a time, you will improve dramatically pretty quickly.

Tip #26

Utilize Your Personal Learning Style

Every person has a style or mode of learning that they are more comfortable with, one that makes it easier for new material to sink in. It is different for everyone, and yet, not much attention is usually paid in school or when studying solo to what mode of learning works best for each individual student.

You may not have much control over how your instructors teach you, but knowing your preferred learning methods may give you a slight advantage. It can help to save time when you are learning by yourself, at least knowing what study methods are most effective for you. Some people learn better visually - either by watching a video, or watching how something is done. Others learn well by listening - maybe listening to audio tapes (iTunes lectures / podcasts or audiobooks). Still others only understand something when they've tried it themselves, they learn by doing. These are broad types - and you could fall anywhere within a spectrum. It doesn't mean other modes of learning don't work for you, it is just that some are easier. There also may be some overlap – combination of styles, or different styles for different subjects.

I am primarily a visual learner. Which means I actually learn best either by reading something myself, or watching someone do something - dance a series of steps, or solve a mathematical problem. I also cannot learn something by simply listening - so audiobooks or lectures without any visual cues are really hard for me, and I hate watching videos where someone is just talking - I lose interest pretty quickly. I figured this out over time - using trial and error. I used to avoid watching videos and lectures online - but then I noticed I don't mind them when there are visuals explaining the material - in fact it's often easier than trying to get the material from a textbook. This means that I can learn a lot faster by choosing the method that works for me best whenever I can. I also learn better through stories than facts, so for learning more about a topic, I try to find books that give context - books that tell a story about a topic. It might mean more work - reading four or five books instead of one, but I can typically read four fun books faster than one tedious one, so it actually saves me time.

There are ways to use this knowledge when you know what style works best for you. If for instance, you're an auditory learner (you work better by listening), you can get the audiobooks of texts you need to read for class, and listen to them on public transport or while driving, or even while walking around, running errands, whatever. You could get lectures on iTunes on topics related to your courses, and listen to them. Some professional exams also have audio lectures available for purchase.

If you're a do-it-yourself learner, try things out for yourself whenever possible. Get home science kits to learn the principles of chemistry and physics for yourself. If you are learning a new programming language, create a website or app. If you are learning accounting, find the annual reports of real companies and look through their income statements and balance sheets. Where you absolutely have to learn something, take your notes and go for a walk, preferably somewhere isolated, and talk your notes to yourself. You may not like to learn sitting quietly at a desk, and may even avoid studying for this reason. Try to find a way to get moving - pace around your room while you learn your work, talk through your arguments for papers before you write them down, use whiteboards and write down facts to memorize or organize ideas for a paper. Find ways to include movement in your study routine so that you have to spend less time sitting at a desk.

For visual learners, the options are endless. Use mind-maps to show the connections between concepts, preferably filled with colors and images. Drawing works for some, but doesn't for others - find out what works for you and use it. Watch videos that walk you through the steps for doing anything - from microeconomics to data analysis to programming. Find timelines and diagrams that explain your topic visually - just do an online search. Or better yet, make your own.

Whatever makes your topics easier to understand and more interesting, is worth spending a bit of time on. As each previously difficult topic becomes clearer, it will shed light on other topics as well. You may find a combination of these strategies work for you, or you may like to watch videos for math but listen to literature on audiobooks. Do whatever works for you, and put aside the other ideas. If you’re not sure what kind of learner you are, or what would work best for a particular subject, try different supplementary materials (see tip #30) to see what might appeal, and even make learning more fun, or at least bearable. The point of this tip is that there isn't one universal method that's perfect for everyone - your teachers may choose whatever is convenient and impose it on the whole class, but you still have options to explore other methods on your own.

Tip #27

Work on Assignments Effectively

As a student, faced with endless assignments, lectures and seminars, extra-curricular activities, part-time jobs and obligations to friends and family, it is understandable that you sometimes (really, most of the time) start studying for tests and quizzes at the last minute. You have a test on Monday, so on Friday evening, you begin to look through your books and notes, and start to read the chapters. Everything seems unfamiliar, there is so much to learn, and it begins to feel a bit overwhelming. Then a friend drops by to chat, or someone calls to invite you a party "where everyone will be there". You decide to stop by, because you're anyway not getting anywhere. You stay out late and wake up tired the next day, but sit down to study for the test anyway. You spend all day at the library - downing four cups of coffee and lots of snacks - pushing yourself to keep going even though your mind is less and less able to focus. Whether studying all-night, or spending all day at the library forcing yourself to cram a semester or half's worth of information in a day - this may seem like the college way of life, but it's incredibly stressful, and actually quite unproductive.

Ideally, you learn in chunks of time, when your mind is fresh, then come back to it again after some time. Now this seems harder, but in reality you will probably be spending the same amount of time studying - but instead of concentrating it all in one day, you will be spreading the work out over time.

Short Writing Assignments

A frequent assignment many students find themselves having to work on are short papers, consisting of a few pages. These aren't the same as larger research papers that account for most of your grade for a particular class (see tip #28 on organizing the process of writing large papers); but those that are due within a few days of being assigned, or discussion papers due at a weekly seminar, asking you to articulate your thinking about a particular topic after doing the assigned reading, or a paper requiring minimal additional research.

To start off, go through the material it is based on and take notes – and maybe type up any passages that you want to quote (with appropriate citations). Start out with a brief outline – it's only a preliminary one and might change – just the points you think you want to make in your paper. This shouldn't take more than 15 minutes. Using the outline, write a rough draft, adding in the quotes you have set aside. Use a freewriting process if you find yourself stuck, just put in anything that you think may be relevant or interesting, which you can edit later.

Preferably save revising for a second session, so that you come to it fresh. This is when you edit, proofread and polish the wording. For a short paper, you usually don't need to spend more than two sessions, and the sessions can be short.

The important thing when writing anything for evaluation is to separate the writing from the editing process, because it makes it much easier to deal with. Even if the separation is short – you work on the first draft, and then break for lunch, and come back and revise it. Also always make an outline, even if it's really basic and changes while you're writing the paper. As discussed in chapter 3 – planning and execution need to be separate, even notionally. It's the same principle behind separating writing and editing, even if the break is a notional one. It's just easier for your mind to do one type of task at a time, rather than juggling multiple tasks – a creative task, what to write next, and an evaluative one, is this expressed in the right way. A large part of procrastination in writing comes from trying to do two different tasks at once, feeling overwhelmed and wanting to avoid that feeling. Breaking up the tasks itself can often be enough to help you stop procrastinating.

Just as in writing larger research papers, the way to make this process easier is to break up the work into steps – reading the primary sources the paper is based on, taking notes on those sources, deciding the outline for your paper, writing it and giving it a final editing and polish. Having a process that you use every time you need to write such a paper, and knowing that you will get the work done without spending a lot of time on it, will help you to feel less anxiety about these frequent writing assignments.

Quantitative Assignments

For assignments in technical courses, you might find yourself lost and this can turn into a source of procrastination. You know that you have trouble with a particular subject, so every week you put off the homework until the night before it's due. Finally, at 10 pm, knowing you absolutely need to work on the assignment, you sit down to work. The assignment consists of six fairly large problems, based loosely on what was covered in class. It takes you an hour to get through half the first problem, at which point you're stuck.

You start the second question, and complete the initial easy sub-parts. Then you find you're stuck on that one too, and have no idea how to even begin the next two questions. At this point it's nearly midnight, you are tired and remembering why you hate this class. You decide to try and get some of the answers from your friend the next day before class and go to bed with a sinking feeling. You can't afford another C on your transcript, but you don't see how to improve. You're doomed.

As discussed earlier (in tip #24), spacing out your studying can help you tackle your schoolwork more easily, by taking advantage of both the focus and diffuse modes in your brain. Trying to cram in an entire assignment in one session, especially for a course you're struggling in, actually makes it much harder to complete the assignment, or improve your understanding of the subject. In order to truly learn the concepts and do well in the tests, you need to be able to develop a good grasp of the topics and be able to apply them to any related problems. If you approach the assignment with the goal of just getting it done as quickly as possible, or try to merely copy the answers from someone without learning the concepts yourself, you will struggle that much more before the exam. It is far better to learn each topic in your course as you go, figuring out for yourself how to solve the problems, correcting your errors and getting the necessary feedback. In short, by *practicing deliberately*. This is best done by approaching your homework in a completely different way.

When you work on a problem, by trying to use everything you have learned so far, including your class notes and your textbook, you invoke the *focus mode* in your brain to solve the problem. If get stuck at any point, you should move on – either to another problem, or some other assignment. In the meantime, your brain's *diffuse mode* is applying itself to the problem, and coming up with insights or ways of approaching it. When after a break you come back to the problem again, you may be able to get the answer to the question, or at least get further along than you were before. At this point, if you are truly stumped and can't get any further on your own, you could approach the teacher or a classmate for assistance, to help you figure out where you're going wrong (see tip #31). In order to go through this process effectively, it is important, therefore, that you don't leave the work until the night before its due if you can help it. Obvious exceptions are homework that is given daily – in that case, break up the work into different sessions, and if you still have doubts, approach your teacher the next day.

By spreading out your study sessions, you come to each session fresh. If you can resolve your doubts and try to keep working till you truly understand each problem, you understand the material better as the semester proceeds, which is crucial because later material usually builds on what you learned initially.

To go back to the previous example - how should you approach the problem set assignment? You are given six problems, and the homework is due in a few days. Set aside an hour or so each over the next couple of days to work on the problems. During these sessions, try every problem, consulting your lecture notes and the textbook for sample problems that are similar to your homework problems. If you get stuck, write down everything you can think of, even if you're not sure or suspect it's wrong. Then move on to the next question. At the second session, try the problems that you got stuck on in the first one – you may have some insights by now. Once you have really given your best shot at all the questions, make an appointment with your instructor or teaching assistant, and go over your doubts with them. After this session, go through the problems again, filling in the blanks. By now you should have a much better grasp of this topic than before.

Group Work

Sometimes you need to work in a group to do tasks that are graded – you are assigned projects, presentations and homework in groups. At times you even write a paper or other final assessment in a group or team. The groups may be formal or informal, such as a regular study group for a particular class. Some courses, usually for quantitative classes, assign problems and either ask or allow you to work in groups.

Many students either shy away from these opportunities or waste the time not knowing how to benefit from it. Serious students who worry about their grades don't often like to work in groups thinking the group will just slow them up or hold them back, or that they might be the ones doing all the work for the entire group. Sometimes that is a legitimate concern - where one person does the work, and others skate off them.

Another way of approaching group work is to simply show up at the designated time, and everyone tries to get through the assignment, or each person does one question, and everyone copies the answer. This latter approach might save time in the short run, but it doesn't help you to actually learn and internalize the concepts to be able to solve problems during the exam.

Many group work sessions can also become excuses to simply hang out and chat, under the guise of work, and not really get a lot done. Sometimes one person, the designated group expert, shows everyone else how to solve the problems, and everyone essentially copies his or her work.

In my modeling class at Cornell, we worked on the assignment in a large group, and two of our classmates helped us out with difficult problems. There is nothing inherently wrong with asking our friends to help us out - but here was the problem - in order to save time, the second any of us got stuck, we asked for help. I didn't really stick with the problem, brainstorming possible ways to answer the question. As a result, I never had the confidence to be able to solve the problems alone in an examination setting, and I didn't feel great about my performance in the final exam for that class. I ended up getting an A because the Professor graded on a curve, but my approach in studying for that class helped to perpetuate the idea in my mind that I wasn't cut out for quantitative subjects because I took the lazy route to completing the homework.

I approached group work quite differently for my economics class. I usually tried to solve the problems by myself first before going to the group session. It might be because I had slightly more confidence in my ability to solve economic problems than modeling ones. I attempted each homework question on my own, trying to work them out till I was genuinely stumped and couldn't figure it out on my own. At the group session, I asked my classmates for help with the areas I was stuck in. By starting the assignment on my own first, I had a much better idea of what my own strengths and weaknesses regarding the material were. I was also able to sometimes help the others with some of the questions - and as we know, teaching others helps to cement knowledge for ourselves. This technique helped me to improve my grasp of economics, and enjoy the more advanced classes when I took them in later semesters. I even got better with each passing week, as concepts generally build on one another, and understanding the initial building blocks helped me to have better familiarity with the later concepts.

So here's what I suggest: if you have homework problems for a quantitative subject and your instructor requires or encourages teamwork - set aside an afternoon (a few hours) or maybe two sessions if you have the time, at least a day before your team meets. Go through the process described earlier regarding quantitative assignments. When you meet with your group, try to get clarifications on what you were stuck on, not just the answers. Make sure that you understand the solutions, don't just blindly copy everything down, and feel free to teach your friends the parts you did understand, it will help to solidify that understanding.

For group work that is non-quantitative, such as study groups for a specific course or project work, follow a similar strategy. Try to summarize or understand the core of the material on your own before you meet with your group. This will help to ensure that the meeting is productive, because you can then focus on what you don't know, or build on your existing knowledge. Even if you do break up the material, with each person responsible for learning and summarizing different parts of the text, ensure that you understand the summaries you get from the others; don't rely on later figuring it out. When you're working with others, the benefit is that someone else can help with your weak spots and vice versa, but it doesn't relieve you of the need to ensure that you have learned the material yourself.

Tip #28

Make Paper Writing Painless

When you need to write a paper, you probably think the writing is the most important part, and get stressed about it, or procrastinate over it. Even when we have weeks to work on something, we keep putting it off till the last moment we possibly can, and then try to write it in one or two long sessions. The experience is absolutely ghastly, and then we dread having to go through it again.

There are obviously many advantages to starting the process much earlier. Starting early gives you more time to think and write something more nuanced, more time to get feedback, even track down important sources. The problem, and the main reason we procrastinate, is that we see writing a paper as one large undifferentiated task. Most of us can get blocked about writing when starting with a blank screen, faced with the prospect of writing thousands of words about a topic we don't know or don't like. The trick is to set up your paper writing process so that you don't have to face a blank screen, and to break up the project into more digestible pieces (see tip #20).

Organize the Writing Process

Paper writing doesn't start with writing; it starts with thinking and organizing. The irony is that you spend weeks avoiding (and stressing) about a task when the part you're avoiding actually comes almost halfway through the project. So even if you are really terrible at writing papers, that is only one aspect of it.

Writing a paper is all about organization – organize your ideas, notes from sources, and then organize the actual writing. Keep track of citations meticulously while you work (all academic programs require you to be very careful when citing someone else's work), and putting together the footnotes and list of references at the end (a hassle-filled task that we usually leave for a couple of hours before submission) will be a snap.

Start the process with a list of everything you need to do. If the paper is more than 50% of your grade for the class, start as early as you can, and set yourself a series of mini-deadlines. Each stage should have a deadline – finalizing a topic, doing research, making an outline, drafting.

Spread the work out in one or two-hour sessions, that way it is far less painful. Some parts of this process can even be fun, especially if you start early enough to not feel stressed. Choose a topic that sounds interesting to you. Even when you are assigned a subject, you can find a way to slant your paper within the broader subject that is more personally appealing to you. This is important - if you have to write a paper anyway, you may as well enjoy the process.

Once you start the research stage, create a folder on your computer where you save documents if they are digital copies or a physical folder for photocopies and printouts. Be sure to carefully label the document with its citation information - it will be painful to have to go hunting for it after you've finished writing the paper.

Write Before You Write

A really useful practice is keeping a journal for the paper. Mystery writer Sue Grafton uses an electronic journal to write down all her thoughts and ideas while writing a novel, keeping a separate journal for each book. Reading about this tip I started to keep a journal for my own large writing projects, and find it an incredibly useful tool. When I'm stuck or not sure which way I need to go, or trying to figure out exactly what I'm trying to say, I sound it out in my journal, and sometimes this can even form the basis for the introduction or other parts of the paper.

Another incredibly useful tip I learned in law school – start writing with a "zero draft". A zero draft is basically an even rougher version of the first draft – where sentences don't necessarily make sense and aren't in order, where ideas are put down but not clearly fleshed out. I usually start with a preliminary outline of some kind, and then put in quotes (labeled with their citations) that I think I might use, and even write a few exploratory paragraphs. The idea is that the more you have to start with before you officially "start writing", the easier it will be to write. Having something to work with, however unpolished, takes the pressure off.

Plan Your Writing First

The easiest way to make progress on paper writing is to break up the different processes of writing and thinking or planning. The mistake students make is to try to do it all at once – you look up a source, or find a quote you want to use, then you try to figure out where in the document it goes. It's incredibly inefficient and actually makes it very hard to make progress. Lack of progress is demoralizing, and underscores the idea that writing a paper is a dreadful task. By separating the different types of tasks you have to do, you actually make it more efficient.

Do this by creating a preliminary outline (this can change), or a mind map, of all the topics and sub-topics you might want to include. This is also a good stage to start to gather the sources and even quotes you might want to include. Advice writer Cal Newport suggests creating a quotes or source document, where you include the quotes that you want to include, under the appropriate headings of your outline. This is a good way to make writing easier for yourself, and to ensure you're not starting from a blank document when you sit down to write. Brainstorm possible sub-topics or points that you will be making in your paper; these will come up from your research, or arise organically from your topic. Make headings for each topic, and put in quotes (labeled carefully with the correct citation) that relate to that topic. When you have done this, even just with your primary sources, you will have something to start with when writing. Ideally, do this with all the sources you plan to consult.

Jump Around In Your Work

Writing a paper doesn't need to be a linear process. We often procrastinate because we think we need to sit down, and write the paper all the way through, and then maybe edit and proofread, and that's it. Thinking this way can cause you to freeze up, because you don't know exactly what to write and how to write it, and basically you get panicky. I've found breaking up the different aspects into separate tasks, and making as much progress as possible on any of the tasks, even if it is out of order, (for instance, you've written something that goes on page 2 and next to it something that goes on page 6) is helpful because just having something to work with cuts down on procrastination.

Keep referring to the list of tasks you made – and if you are stuck and can't make progress on writing the paper, pick some other task that is doable – for instance, working on the bibliography. Jump around and do the easiest parts first, and follow the tips on procrastination in chapter 5.

Try to complete a draft early on, to get feedback from your Professor or the writing center. Also, leave plenty of time for editing. Acknowledge to yourself that your first draft doesn't have to be perfect - what matters is that you write something so that you have something to work on, like having some clay to mold. That's why it is the first draft. If you want, save it on your computer with a name that makes it clear that it's a first draft – such as Essay_Oliver Twist 1.0.docx. That's what I do with all large projects or when I'm completely frozen - this is a signal to my brain that this is just a first attempt, there will be plenty more.

When you organize and plan the writing process, it leaves you room for more time to think, by starting earlier and by reducing the stress and general panic you would feel from putting it off. Noodling in your process journal, thinking about the ideas you have read, you might come up with interesting insights on the material, or a new way of thinking or organizing the ideas. This is what can really transform your grade.

Chapter 7
Tackling Difficult Subjects

"The real struggle in life is with ourselves. The true secret of success is the refusal to give up, the refusal to fail; it lies in the struggle to win the battle against one's own weaknesses."

– Dr. Daisaku Ikeda

Almost all students are weak at least in one subject, and frequently in more than one. Fortunately, there are many strategies that can help you to improve your weaker areas. In conjunction with the strategies in the previous chapters, the advice in this chapter focuses on ways to turn your grades around in courses where you're lagging behind.

Tip #29

Isolate Your Weaknesses

When you're struggling with a particular subject at school, it can seem hopeless that you can ever turn it around. You have been getting poor grades for so long, you start to believe that it's you, that you just aren't cut out for that subject, whether it is math or a language or history. You might be tempted to give up, to say to yourself "I will never catch up", or that "I'm not smart enough to do this". I used to feel like that about computer science – we had a teacher who didn't really explain things very well, or even teach us the basics. Most of my classmates already knew a lot about computers and programming, so her job was made pretty easy. I was, however, completely clueless, staring blankly at the screen with no idea how to start. I was also doing pretty badly in math and physics at the time, not understanding a word in class, and cribbing the homework off a friend, not because I was too lazy to try, but because the gaps in my understanding were so wide, I couldn't even attempt the assignments.

One thing years of school and college, and repeatedly tackling subjects I had no idea about initially, has taught me is that any subject can be mastered. It's not you; it's your study strategy. If you don't understand the basics, skipping to the more advanced material just makes you incredibly confused and start to doubt yourself. If you are willing to put in the hard work, no gap in knowledge is insurmountable.

Start by really looking at your courses, and making a list of which areas you're struggling in. Don't just say – math or physics. Be specific. Which topics do you not understand at all? Or conversely, which ones do you find easy? Many things in school build on one another – so if you skipped something earlier, then all the subsequent topics are a blur as well. When that happened to me in school I just assumed I didn't have a "math brain", despite getting the top marks in class in math for years previously. It turns out, all you need to do is go backward, and try to untangle where exactly it stopped making sense. When you're first embarking on improving your grades in certain subjects, you may not know where to start. After all, it's a subject you're not good at. However, in order to get better, you need to know, what are the issues?

You might start to think at this point that you will need to study all the time in order to make any progress, and still not get through everything. This is especially the case if you follow the next tip, and gather question banks, study guides and online tutorials; you may end up with a mountain of primary and supplementary material for your study prep. The goal isn't to get through every video or app out there, the goal is to improve your grade, and conquer your specific weaknesses. So let's take a step back before you embark on the actual studying to ask yourself, what do you really need to focus on?

If you're prepping for an exam, the best way to use the supplementary material is to isolate and eliminate your main weaknesses. So first, identify what they are. If you have already taken exams for this course, which concepts or sections of the paper did you find most difficult or get most questions wrong? In history - is it the dates and details, or the essays? In math, is it solving the steps correctly, or knowing how to interpret word problems into numbers? Or is it that you're really slow during a test, and can't complete the questions in time? If you haven't taken any exams yet, focus on which topics of the course so far you had the most difficulty understanding. Use any practice tests and assignments, or even just a reading of your textbook, to point you in the right direction. Make a comprehensive list of everything you can think of, because knowing the problem makes it easier to tackle.

Once you have a list, go through it systematically. Look through your material and isolate whatever will help you to eliminate or reduce these weaknesses. Maybe a textbook that simplifies the material can help with the concepts in economics you don't really get. Or an online course can clarify your physics understanding. If you're struggling with French spelling, set aside time every day, maybe while commuting to school, to go through some modules on an app. In some subjects, you need to go logically – in science and math you get harder subjects later in the course, so if you're struggling, go back to the initial topics and solidify your understanding. Identifying what you need to focus on most provides a filter through everything you need to get done, and when in a time-crunch, focus on these areas first, because improving here will show the greatest difference in your grades.

This may seem pretty obvious, but you'll be surprised how many students (including me) have failed to take this approach. It's much easier to work on what you like and are good at, than on something you don't understand. Studying isn't always pleasant anyway, why make it worse by wrestling with binomials and differentials when you can just re-read your history textbook or re-learn those names for French food, right? Well, that's understandable, but unfortunately a losing study strategy. If you want to cut short the amount of time you spend over your books, or dramatically increase your GPA, you need to ruthlessly identify the areas you're weakest in, the questions that you always get wrong, or the concepts that you nod along to in class and memorized the formula for, but if needed to teach it to someone else, you wouldn't be able to get past the first sentence. Simply learning many concepts aren't enough if the questions test more subtle understanding, for example, graphs that often need you to really know the concepts cold, or MCQs that pick on the trickiest aspects of the material.

For courses that focus less on testing, and instead are based on writing a paper, or submitting a project, you need to tweak this approach slightly. If paper-writing is something you're good at, that's great. But if not, plan to start a lot earlier, so that you have plenty of time to get feedback on your work. Analyze your previous work and try to assess (or ask your teachers) where you are weakest - is it that the research isn't in-depth enough, or is it your structure? Or do you need to improve your proofreading skills? Once you know what steps trip you up - you can focus on getting help.

If you are having trouble with research, don't simply start with a search engine - ask the school librarian. They can often point out better and more targeted sources for your topics. If your structure needs work, try to get help from the school writing center, if available. If you're not sure about your topic, run it by your Professor. Ask your friends to proofread your work - sometimes a fresh perspective is needed to catch errors. You can increase your grades by being honest with yourself about the aspects of your courses you have the greatest difficulties in, and try to find ways to shore up those weaknesses.

Tip #30

Use Supplementary Materials

Sometimes we don't understand a subject - maybe we missed too many days of school due to illness and are behind, or didn't pay attention, or our teachers don't explain the concepts clearly (or as it happened to me, we changed four teachers in one year, which threw off my learning completely). In these circumstances, telling yourself you are doing badly in the subject because you are stupid or just not destined to get it is counter-productive (see tip #29). Even when it seems hopeless, there are ways you can improve your understanding of a particular subject, and the best way to do it is to get some supplementary materials to help you.

The last thing you probably want to do is get more books or other materials to add to the work you have to do. If you're already struggling with your homework, the idea that you have to voluntarily go out and get more to do probably sounds crazy. Before you put the book (or e-reader) down in disgust, just bear with me for a moment. Imagine how it would feel to sit for a test, read through the question paper, open up your answer booklet and confidently start to write answers to the questions? Or to be able to sit down to do your homework knowing that you can handle most of it on your own, knocking it off in an hour or two, leaving enough time to have some guilt-free fun because you have completed your work?

It's faster and less stressful to study and do assignments and study for tests when you actually know what you're doing, when you understand the material, and it's not just one big mass of words in a foreign language you don't understand. When you're struggling with a particular subject, it is understandable to want to spend less time with it, not more. However, the best way to get better at it is to approach the material in different ways, become more familiar with it, and simply get a different perspective.

Sometimes working from different angles can help to improve your understanding. Scott Young, an expert at self-learning, calls this "supplying the missing pieces". Use the supplementary materials to complement your weaknesses and fill in the missing pieces in your understanding. As you commit to finding and eliminating these areas, it's a bit like a video game, and as you get better and rack up more points, you 'level up'.

There are many types of supplementary materials, some will appeal more to you or be more suitable for you than others, depending on what's available and what works for you. Feel free to experiment and try different approaches.

Study Guides

For most subjects, there are many books that explain the concepts simply, highlighting the key points or giving simpler examples to follow. For instance, the *Demystified* series of books is one I recommend highly; I went through a few recently and was able to learn how to tackle math problems that I struggled to master in high school and while prepping for the GRE exam. The books are particularly useful because they break each topic down into steps of increasing difficulty, providing numerous worked-out examples, to show you how to do the different types of problems. As you master one level of difficulty, you then move to slightly harder problems. If you're struggling in a particular technical subject at school, try to find similar guides that contain many worked-out problems and lots of practice problems. It might take longer to do this extra work, but it will quickly help you close those gaps in your understanding, making it easier to follow along in class, do your homework and do better in tests.

The reason this tactic, of breaking down concepts and practicing lots of problems of increasing difficulty, works so well in improving your understanding of technical subjects is that it is the best way to form a *chunk* of that concept, using *deliberate practice* (see tip #24). As you go through the problems on your own, and then check your work with the solutions, you are straining to reach for knowledge that is just outside your grasp, as well as getting instant feedback on your efforts. This process mirrors the best way for your brain to learn and therefore helps to solidify the information in your mind, ready to use when needed.

For non-technical subjects, study guides can help in two ways. They can condense the material, so that you focus on first understanding and learning the foundational aspects, making it easier to then add on more complex knowledge. For many subjects in the humanities and social science, there is literally a book's worth of information to get through on every topic within the subject. This can all start to seem very overwhelming. A study guide can help to identify the core of the material, and once you master the core, you can return to the original materials and use them to add to the picture. Think of it like building a house. The study guides can help create a scaffolding, maybe even add on the walls and ceiling, so now you have a bare structure of ideas in place. Then going back to the in-depth readings, you can start to add the flooring and paint and put in the windows.

In law school when I was really struggling with certain topics like constitutional law, I borrowed some books from the local library that were simplified guides, and explained the legal principles in simple language, with fewer examples. This helped me to get a good overview of the subject, and then I went back to my textbooks to learn the finer points.

The second way that study guides can help is by arranging critical aspects of the topic in ways that make it easier to learn. For instance, guides for literature generally discuss the themes of the work, and provide examples of symbolism and other literary devices employed in the text. Many guides aimed at law students condense important cases into a few paragraphs that highlight the crucial elements and points of law, and even create outlines so that you can easily see how different aspects of the topic relate to one another.

Software

Another supplementary material that can be really helpful is software targeted to your subject. Educational software usually is easier to learn from because they typically include audio/visual components and interactive materials. Sometimes they can include interesting extra facts, extra practice tests or simply more in-depth explanations of topics.

In law school I studied extensively from a CD-ROM that contained the basics of many of our core topics - contract, tort, administrative and property law (our Professors recommended it). The software presented the main points of each topic, with summaries of the most important cases, and links to supplementary materials. I used that CD-ROM as a starting point for many courses, and even as a revision aid.

Textbooks in law school can comprise of several hundred pages and contain a lot of detail. The software helped because it provided a high-level view of the topic, with only a few selected cases or statutes described in detail. Sometimes you can be so overwhelmed in details, the big-picture completely eludes you, and it's hard to get a handle on how things fit together. I realized it was much easier to start with the software's overview of the topic, and then move on to my textbooks.

Some technical textbooks come with a CD-ROM as part of a package. The ones that are extremely useful contain extra practice material with solutions; some even use games with different levels to induce you to actually go through the problems. Other software that can be really helpful as an additional study aid are language learning ones like Rosetta Stone. Some of them can be extremely expensive, so if you have access to it through your local or school library, try it out to see if it helps you. Not everyone finds it equally useful, some programs are suited mostly for solidifying basic vocabulary and grammar. For instance, the basic way the Rosetta Stone works is to immerse you in the target language, without using English. Instead it uses pictures, and you learn the words in context as you progress through the lessons. The additional advantage of Rosetta Stone is also that audio is explicitly part of the program - and speaking and hearing is also tested, unlike in some apps and other programs, where although audio is provided, it's not one of the skills evaluated. Again it's a matter of determining how you learn best, and trying to incorporate different methods into your study routine - to improve different skills and also to keep it fresh.

Online Apps

For learning many subjects, there are a ton of free and paid apps that you can download to your phone or tablet. If you don't own a smartphone, or just want other options, there are also downloadable software and / or web-based applications that you can use. The applications available cover a range of topics - languages, vocabulary for standardized tests, history facts, cases for the bar exam; the list is endless. You can choose what works for you, and also focus on your own weaknesses, so that you can find an extra way to practice.

For example, while prepping for the verbal component of the GRE, I got bored just flipping through my flashcards, so I searched for online prep materials (I didn't have a smartphone then) and I found some websites that allowed reinforced the vocabulary through games you could play online.

There are apps and online games that utilize the concept of *spaced repetition* (see tip #24) to help you remember all sorts of information from French verbs to economic phenomena. You go through the flashcards or images or questions, and answer as many of them as you can. Then the next time you practice, the app will show you the questions that you had trouble with more often than the ones you got easily. You do this a few more times, and you are sure to remember what you learned for a long time, and do it with less effort than it takes to sit there stubbornly for hours, trying to memorize a semester's worth of information in a couple of days. You can even download free software to your computer that lets you make your own flashcards with whatever info you need to learn, and then go through the cards in this manner - going through them with a few days interval. Anki is one such program that you can download, and it also has a web-based version. The cards you have the most difficulty with will come up more frequently - so you, in essence, get a personally tailored test that shows you what you're struggling with, and helps you to learn them.

In recent years, there are a few apps that I've found incredibly useful. A free app, Memrise, is great for learning languages, and also for learning other subjects. It also uses the concept of spaced repetition, to help you revise the words or concepts that you have the most difficulty with more often. You can create your own database, but I just used many of the excellent pre-existing resources. It's especially excellent for languages - I used it to start learning Chinese characters, and made really good progress for a while, but finally gave it up because I didn't have the time to keep up the practice.

A paid app that I really liked using is Mindsnacks. It is mostly for learning languages (they have versions for French, Spanish, Italian and a few others). It has its drawbacks - for instance, I'm not sure how great it would be for learning a tonal language like Mandarin, but it is great as a beginner to intermediate companion for vocabulary. It shines in helping you get a lot of practice with basic vocabulary, practicing spelling and learning simple grammar. The interesting games make it easy to spend time practicing and developing skills in your target language, and you can progress from complete beginner to an intermediate to advanced stage. If you're looking to lock in basic grammar and gain mastery of a few thousand words in your target language without memorizing word lists, this app and others like it are a good choice, as they provide yet another way to get *deliberate practice* in the basic skills of your target language.

You can find games and apps that help you get practice learning most subjects, and some even allow you to create personalized flashcards. In fact, the only drawback to this tactic is that the sheer volume of options available can be overwhelming. Remember, the goal is to actually practice whatever you are trying to learn, not spend several hours finding the "perfect" app or game. To ensure that you don't waste time, try to use these tools for those aspects of your study that you know you need extra practice in, and stop or move on to something else when you've mastered the knowledge.

Videos

A great way to get additional help for your courses, get a different perspective, and even learn a skill that isn't taught at your school but might help something you're learning about or want to learn about, is watching videos online. There are videos online (many for free) that teach the fundamentals of an increasing number of subjects, and some universities even make full courses available for free.

Many top universities like Yale and MIT have posted entire courses online on Youtube - where you can watch the videos and learn the material. They have courses on a wide variety of subjects, and although there are usually no other materials available besides the videos (some courses make problem sets and solutions available), it is a great resource if you just want an overview of a subject area or need to brush up your skills. I watched the Yale Environmental Law course uploaded on Youtube, and not only did I acquire a better understanding of the interaction between law and environment, it really helped me when I was working on a project not long after, where one of the big components was environmental law and politics.

If you're trying to improve your understanding of certain technical subjects, and find there are specific gaps in your understanding, or you just need another perspective, try Khan Academy, which is a free resource with videos and practice problems. If you sign up, you can also get personalized problems - so you work at your own level, and as you improve in your understanding, you get tougher problems. This can be a great way to improve at your own pace, and gives you personalized *deliberate practice*.

Organizations like Coursera, Udacity and edX offer free (with additional priced features) courses that are called MOOCs (mass online open courses). They have tied up with prestigious universities worldwide to provide courses in most subjects that anyone can take. Most courses follow the format of traditional university courses - with a syllabus, reading list and lectures in the form of videos. There are so many courses, you are sure to find something to complement what you're already studying, explain it from a different perspective, or add to your knowledge. The courses try to make the subject as interesting as possible, using examples of more current and global issues.

Knowing more about a topic, or being able to provide context helps to make it more engaging, and that also helps you learn and remember more. We remember whatever we have strong emotions towards, or can associate with something memorable. You're going to find it very difficult to remember anything said in class if you're bored and only half-paying attention. Learning can be a lot of fun, with the right instructor and approach - using examples, showing diagrams, referencing something interesting that is current and linking that to the topic. You might not be able to change your teachers in school, but you can get some additional ones online, many of them for free.

Watch Movies

This may be a controversial suggestion, seeming more like a procrastination strategy or something that only slacker students indulge in. Bear with me for this one. If you are assigned books to read that have been made into movies, or if there are movies related to your subject area or topic, watch them. Yes, this is a legitimate study technique, albeit with some guidelines.

Firstly, this is NOT a substitute for thoroughly reading the original text, especially for courses where you have to analyze the subject matter more closely or quote from the text. Secondly, don't wait for the night before your paper on *Great Expectations* or *Hamlet* is due to watch the movie. Again, this isn't a strategy to save you from doing the actual work of reading and analyzing the work, and writing an original and well-thought out paper.

So what's the benefit then? Well, firstly, it's a great way to take a break from intense periods of studying. You can watch the movie or documentary when you're too tired to do any focused work. Also, the change of medium can be very helpful if you're a visual learner. (For auditory learners, consider additionally listening to the audiobook - you can do this during your commute, while walking, doing errands.) Personally, I find watching the film adaptations of some of my favorite novels and plays actually bring them to life in a completely different way than my own imagination. Depending on the adaptation, the costumes and the delivery of the actors help to put the words into context, remember them better and even get a more nuanced understanding of the story and the characters. If there are several adaptations, watch as many as you have access to and have time for. In fact, watching the adaptation of *An Ideal Husband* by Oscar Wilde made me return to the play wanting to read it (I love his work, but never finished reading that particular play).

Watching a movie is a different sensory experience from

reading, and can help you to remember dialogue, understand the emotional temperature of the characters and spot themes that may be more difficult to do when reading the book or play. This is probably a more fun suggestion than some of the others, but don't think that it is any less effective. I had never watched any of Jane Austen's books adapted for the screen when I studied them in school, and had to read the texts several times to get a better idea of the whole. Subsequently, I've seen many adaptations, and each one helped me to gain a richer understanding of the work and its themes.

Language Practice

Let's say you are learning French. What is more appealing? Listening to tapes and reading grammar books, or talking to a native speaker? You might not be confident about your language ability, but one or two sessions with a native speaker could improve your French (or whatever language you're learning) much faster than hours of drills on your own. You could make a huge leap in your understanding and confidence about the language. That, in turn, would come across in your tests, as well as in your motivation to study.

There are services online that let you pay for an hour of conversation, or even exchange language learning practice for free with someone who speaks your target language and wants to learn your mother tongue (or whatever language you are fluent in). You could also watch movies in your target language, or listen to podcasts or music. The idea is to basically find different ways to stimulate your interest in the language as well as increasing your exposure to it.

Tip #31

Ask for Help

Even after you have tried using study guides or watched a bunch of videos, you still may be struggling with certain aspects of your courses. Maybe your subjects are more specialized and there isn't a lot of supplementary material available. Or perhaps you just need a bit more targeted assistance. Once you have tried to learn on your own, and isolated exactly where you are struggling, this is the time to ask for help.

Reaching Out

When we don't feel very comfortable with a subject, we often also find it hard to ask for help. Perhaps we worry that our inadequacies may be revealed - the Professor, the teaching assistant or our classmate will know the extent of what we don't know. Perhaps we think the amount of help we need is a lot, more than the person we ask is prepared to give us. Perhaps we are just shy or think that those we ask will not want to help. Some teachers or classmates aren't very responsive, but many people are happy to explain something you're struggling with, or even advice you on other sources of help. According to Panagiotis, a former honors student in Computer Science, you shouldn't be shy about asking for help, because "after all, the Professors are there to help you and they are obliged by the institution to answer your questions until you are satisfied with and you have understood the answer".

Asking questions also helps your classmates. If your Professor is going really fast, and you don't understand something, asking for clarification can slow down the pace and help everyone to catch up. Student mentor Dr. Margaret Reese says, "If you failed to understand a concept in the previous lecture, odds are very good your classmates did not understand it either. Asking the first question can encourage others to ask questions and slow the pace further".

The timing and context of the assistance asked for is also important. The best way to benefit from approaching someone for help with a specific homework assignment or problems with conceptual understanding is preparation. Firstly, it is best to start by asking for assistance on something very specific - like a homework problem set or help with understanding a graph or example from the lecture. This is useful for two reasons: it enables you to overcome your awkwardness and start off with a simpler request, and it helps the person helping you to have something specific to focus their attention on, and to know that their time outlay is limited. When you're comfortable with this sort of query, you might also ask the person for more general advice – perhaps regarding essay-writing, or ask for recommendations for supplementary materials.

Making the Request

So how do you go about asking for help? Most Professors and even some TAs have office hours - you can email them or just show up. Emailing in advance is helpful because they know you are coming, and that helps if the person's office hours are particularly popular.

If they don't have office hours, you can just send an email and request a meeting. Sometimes you can even address your query directly in the email itself - which saves time and helps if you are really shy or unsure about approaching them in person. For one of my classes in graduate school, we had to write computer programs as part of our assignments. When my programs didn't work, even though I thought I had understood the question and had a good understanding of the solution, I emailed the Professor with the code (the programs were usually very short, only a few lines). He could look at the email at his own convenience and get back to me, which he usually did pretty quickly. This was also helpful to demonstrate that I was trying, and often even when the program didn't work, I got credit for the effort.

Asking for help enables your instructors to know that you put in the effort, and they will be more likely to give you the benefit of the doubt when you make mistakes in your work, and also will be more inclined to help you in the future. We all like to believe that educators are impartial and see everyone equally, but unfortunately, that's not always the case. Those students who ask for help and who look like they are making an effort, are the ones who receive more assistance.

Preparing in Advance

The best way to prepare for office hours is also the same strategy I recommend for group work. In classes where group work is not permitted or discouraged, you might find yourself lost with the assignments and this can turn into a source of procrastination. Try to work through the assignment on your own first, even if you can only complete half of the problem set, or create a very rough outline of the essay you have to write. Be as prepared as you can be, putting in writing absolutely everything you can do on the assignment. Seeing your process of thinking can be helpful to your instructor when you later go over the work together.

Make an appointment to see your Professor or TA as early as you can. Try to resolve as many of the doubts as you can, if possible, work through the problems with them, and show them where you got stuck. Usually your Professor or Teaching Assistant will be able to guide you towards the solution, even if they don't give you an outright answer. Or they can simply help you get unstuck, or see where your mistake in reasoning was, or clarify an assumption. Then schedule a study session as soon after as possible, preferably the same day while the conversation is fresh, to go over your work and make the suggested changes. Neatly write or type up your assignment. Even if you still don't get every question right, you should be doing much better.

In graduate school, while studying game theory, I routinely had trouble with the problem sets. I tried the problems on my own, and invariably got stuck on 80% of them - either because I didn't fully understand the question, or just didn't know how to convert the word problem to a game which I could solve. I regularly attended office hours to work through my doubts, after going through every problem on my own. I was able to clarify my doubts as the term progressed instead of waiting till just before exams, and I realized that I actually knew more than I thought I did, drastically reducing my stress levels. I started to really enjoy the subject, and did much better than I expected on the exams and the final project. I also developed a good relationship with the Professor, who gave me advice on other courses and recommendations when I needed them.

Tip #32

Dig Beneath Your Feet

Feeling Overwhelmed About The Work

When you are really behind in a particular course, thinking about improving your grades or the amount of work you need to do, it may seem really overwhelming. You can feel like you are standing at the bottom of a mountain looking up, and the climb to the top looks awfully steep and far away. It's not unusual to feel like this at all, in fact it's pretty common. You have thought about and isolated your weaknesses in the subjects you're taking, you have gathered a bunch of supplementary materials to go through, and you are convinced that theoretically it's possible to change your grade if you put in the effort. But at this point it all seems a bit too much, there is so much to do, so little time, and you really aren't sure whether you can do it all. You don't even know where to start.

Think back to a time when you took up an activity that you love, but weren't necessarily always good at. Maybe you wanted to join the basketball team at school. Did you give up, say it's impossible, or did you determine that no matter what, you would improve and get good enough to join the team? Maybe you stayed behind after school, or woke up early morning to practice. Once you got better, you kept increasing your practice and efforts till finally, you made it on to the team.

The same method can be applied to studying, even though you probably like basketball, but don't like to study. The thing is, the better you get at something, the more you enjoy it. Maybe you started to love basketball after you made a few shots in the basket, or won a friendly game with your friends. Liking school can be similar - once you start to get the hang of it, you begin to like it more. Even if you never really look forward to studying, it can be less hateful. And being good at anything, whether it is sports or art or mathematics, gives you confidence in yourself, and a sense of accomplishment that is hard to replicate.

During my Master's program, I took a course on international trade. It was a small class, and I was really interested in the topic, but I didn't understand a word the Professor spoke. He used a lot of jargon and wrote incomprehensible equations on the board. Most of the other students were economics majors, there were even a few PhD candidates, and they understood the Professor's shorthand and obscure references, but I didn't since I had only taken one or two economics classes before. The syllabus hadn't indicated that it would be very quantitative focused, and I really wanted to learn the material. I panicked, realizing that I needed to either understand the lectures or drop the class.

Another Professor guided me to some good introductory materials available online, and I started to learn about the fundamentals of international trade. I took meticulous notes, studying late at night after completing my homework in other subjects. As I started to understand the basics, I worked through the entire reading list for the class, tracking down every journal article or book on the syllabus and taking notes on the material. I still hadn't begun to understand the lectures, but I started to recognize a few phrases and side comments.

All the hard work paid off, however, as I ended up getting the highest grade in class on both the midterm and the final exam, by a wide margin. Turns out the Professor based the exam questions mostly on the assigned reading, and apparently I was one of the few who had so diligently read it. I also learned a lot about a fascinating and important subject.

Starting With Where You Are

Whenever I get overwhelmed by how much I have to do, or how behind I am, I remind myself to "dig beneath my feet". The phrase comes from advice given by my mentor, Dr. Daisaku Ikeda - "Dig beneath your feet, there you will find a spring" - which basically means to start with where you are, without worrying about how far you need to go, or whether where you are is really the perfect place. Make a list of everything you need to do, and start with the first thing. Start anywhere, with whatever is in front of you. The key is to begin - and to trust that as long as you're putting one foot in front of the other, eventually you'll get to where you need to, or at the very least, much farther than you had initially imagined.

Digging beneath your feet also means not to look at others, or compare to them. After all, you're busy looking downward, at your own small patch of ground. You don't have the time to look around at your neighbors, to see what fruit their patches have borne. The unfortunate reality of life is that it's practically woven into our DNA, this desire to compare. With modern technology and social media, this is even easier to do. But since we never compare to someone who is worse off than us, we inevitably feel terrible as a result of this comparison. Maybe you have a friend who barely does his assignments, dashing them off last minute, and he is always goofing off in classes. But he consistently gets straight-As. Or maybe you and a friend are studying for a test, and she doesn't seem to know the material as well as you do. However, she does better than you on the test. This can seem totally unfair, and you might say to yourself, "Why do I even bother putting in any effort when it's all random?" The thing is, it's not random. Perhaps your friend who is goofing off at school, really studies hard at home. Maybe your friend has good test-taking abilities and performs well under pressure. Comparing can be demoralizing, especially since you may not have the full picture. It is far more productive to simply focus on what you can do.

When I was prepping for my 10th grade board exams in high school, I had to pull up my grades in almost all my subjects - in some cases up from 40 or 50%. I was working really hard, but still only making modest progress. I improved in every subject, but while I might be getting a 70% in most of my subjects (a 20% increase), some of my classmates got 90%, usually in a subject they found effortlessly easy. I used to get frustrated and complain to my parents, because it felt like I was trying to run in water. My dad gave me some really good advice then, which has helped me later in life as well. He said, "Your friends are doing really well in one subject, playing to their strengths and ignoring their weaknesses. You are focusing on shoring up your weaknesses, improving in every subject, so it looks less impressive. Give it some time and you'll surpass them". At the time I didn’t believe I could even reach close to the same level. But I kept at it, kept focusing on what was in front of me, whatever I needed to get done that day. Eventually I got the highest grades that year; but more importantly, I was able to go far beyond what I thought was possible, which felt even better than comparing to others.

Chapter 8
Revising For Exams

"I've missed more than 9000 shots in my career.

I've lost almost 300 games. 26 times, I've been

trusted to take the game winning shot and missed.

I've failed over and over and over again in my life.

And that is why I succeed."

– Michael Jordan

Taking tests is anxiety-inducing - and many students think that they are simply poor at taking tests, that they don't have what it takes. Test-taking is a skill like everything else, it can be learned, and improved upon. Part of the anxiety associated with taking a test comes from the feeling that you don't know what is coming and how you will do. It can feel like gambling, without the fun and possibility of winning money. The best way to combat this feeling is to know that you're well-prepared - by learning the material, testing yourself on it, and taking practice tests if available.

Most students who are good at taking exams have strategies and routines they follow. This chapter gives tips and strategies that I recommend when preparing for a test. The most important takeaway however, is that this is merely the last step; improving your study habits at every stage ensures that you have built the best possible foundation to confidently enter this last stage and do your best.

Tip #33

Practice The Skills You Will Need

What Will You Be *Really* Tested On?

It's really crucial to actually practice the skill(s) you will need or be tested on. What is the format of the assessment, and hence what skills will you need to stand out? Is it learning by rote? Knowing how to turn word problems into equations, and then solving those correctly? Essays critiquing a text?

Athletes and other elite performers practice the exact skill that they will need. For instance, pro golfers like Tiger Woods practice getting their ball out of a sand trap, even when it is an exceedingly rare occurrence because if they don't practice, on the actual day of the competition, they will not be able to pull it off. It's the same for taking a test – even when you may have studied generally for a specific subject, if you don't know how to approach the questions, you will struggle and may fail to do well despite working hard.

In law school, even though I knew the cases and the legal principles, I didn't know how to answer the questions in a way that fit what the examiner was looking for. I crammed for hours and could recite all the case law, but ultimately I did poorly in many of my exams in the first year because I didn't know that there was a technique to answering the questions, that it was more subtle than just writing down the legal principles involved. After studying so hard, I was confused when my results were lackluster, but later realized I had been preparing for the exam incorrectly.

Similarly, for the essay section of the GRE, prep books tell you exactly how to approach it, and what points to hit. Although most of us can write essays, there is a method that is more effective, and garners higher grades. So it is really beneficial to know in advance what the specific skill is that we need to know for a particular exam, and then practicing that skill. Blindly jumping in to study for a test without first figuring out what the format is, and what skills will be tested causes many students to do badly in exams, and then assume that they can't do well in tests.

Why Practice Is Important

The reason practice is so crucial is that you can fool yourself, thinking that you know how to solve the problems, or answer the test questions. However, answering questions in an exam actually consist of a number of skills, closely linked. To get more efficient at them, just like at any other skill, you need practice. In tests where you have to answer a lot of questions within a tight time constraint, spending an extra 20 - 30 seconds thinking about how to approach the question, or trying to remember a formula, can add up to several minutes used up, which might lose you valuable points if you can't complete the test. Ideally, you want to practice to the point where you can look at a question and know without hesitation how to answer it. This gives you a valuable buffer for the eventuality that there will be some questions where you are truly stumped - giving you a bit more time to work on them, and even if you have to simply hazard a guess, you won't be as badly off.

By practicing what you're actually tested on, you hone that skill, develop confidence and calm your nerves. If we refer to the concept of *deliberate practice* again, the more you replicate the action you need to take or the specific skill you want to master, under the specific conditions that you will face, the more comfortable you will be with repeating that action when it counts. In the context of playing golf, that might mean getting used to playing under tournament conditions, when you have to train yourself not to get distracted by the spectators. In studying, that might mean making sure you can complete the test within the time allotted, and not letting the pressure of the situation overwhelm you so much that your mind goes blank.

So how do you approach this process? Adapt your study strategy to the kind of test you're facing, instead of just vaguely reading the textbook and your notes, hoping that somehow you will be able to imbibe this knowledge and replicate it in the test. The format of the exam will guide your revision strategy. Is it multiple choice, or essay based? Are any sample exams available? You don't need to solve them - but just glance at them so you know what you're aiming for. It starts to cue in your mind what you're looking for when studying.

Try to set up some of your study time to do a timed practice test, or several if you can, sticking to the time you will have for the real thing. The more crucial the exam you are preparing for (or the more unfamiliar the format), the more you should try to practice. Many things can still go wrong on test day – the more you can turn your specific knowledge into skills that you have already practiced, the easier it is to get good grades despite things not going according to plan.

How Practicing A Skill Helped Me Ace An Exam

In high school, almost against the advice of my parents, I took an advanced English literature class. My parents were concerned that it would be hard to get a good grade, and it would affect my overall GPA. I was, however, determined to take this particular class. I really loved the class, but I found myself floundering pretty early on - even though I tried really hard, I always received each paper I wrote returned with a lot of red ink all over it, and a barely passing grade. I didn't know how to study for this class, but I decided to figure out a way to improve my work.

I started with any books I could find in the school library, and also looked online for critical evaluations and study guides for the novels and poems we were meant to be studying. We had to study several novels, plays and around 50 poems each year, and be prepared to critically evaluate each work, and the final exam (which counted for the entire grade) was entirely essay-based. There weren't any past exam papers or model answers available, but I had a good idea from class assignments what was expected. I was well-prepared for the novels and plays, but was still quite nervous about the poems, and a few days before the exam, I started to panic. After I complained to my father that all of the secondary material I had read was overwhelming me, he suggested I write an essay for each poem. I was reluctant to do so much work, with only a few days of prep left, but I decided to do it anyway.

Over the next few days, I wrote around 50 essays, giving myself a time limit of 30 - 40 minutes for each essay. Writing the essays mirrored the principles of deliberate practice, because I had to get used to writing analytical essays under a timed situation, using quotes from the text to support my analysis. The work definitely paid off, because I received a 97% grade in that exam, the highest in my class and in the history of that course in my school.

Tip #34

Create A Personal Study Guide

Studying for an exam can be overwhelming - you don't know where to start. You have lecture notes, assignments, notes from your reading, past exam papers. Where do you start when you only have a few weeks before an upcoming exam?

A good starting point is creating a personal study guide as you go through the semester or term. This will be the place where you put information that is pre-digested, i.e. already analyzed, and ready to be learned for your test. The purpose of the study guide is to have a personalized set of notes that contain all the most important things you need to learn in order to do well in the test – whether they are concepts to be applied, facts to be memorized or arguments that you need to know and be able to critique. Just gathering the information isn't effective, ideally you need to engage with it in some form to be able to internalize it and apply it when needed.

The study guide can be in whatever format suits you - a Microsoft Word document, a notebook in Microsoft OneNote or Evernote, a physical binder with printed (or handwritten) notes, or even a set of books and preparatory materials. Just make sure it is in a format that is useful to you, easy to access and update. Also remember to back it up regularly, or store it in a cloud-based application like Dropbox.

What goes in the study guide? Well this depends on what your exam format is, and what you have to learn. You can include lists of vocabulary / terminology / definitions; formulae that you need to solve problems; worked-out sample exam questions. Any practice problems provided by your teacher, or sets of sample questions that you plan to work on your own may also be included. The summaries that you made of your research papers / articles from your reading should also go into this guide (see tip

#25). As I said earlier, creating these summaries as you go through the course will save you a ton of time later. The same method can be used to summarize economic or business theories or case studies. The summaries help you to learn the main points of each topic and see how they fit together across the subject. Once you have learned the key points, they should help you trigger enough details as required.

The study guide could also contain timelines and maps that you create - tying in concepts and events peppered through the subject. It may be tempting to simply copy these from the textbook if they are available, or Google your topic for ready-made diagrams - and while that can be a useful supplementary aid - I suggest you spend the time making the mental connections yourself, in whatever form. Feel free to use colors, images, write in shorthand - the guide is for you, so it only needs to make sense to you. This is also a great place to create metaphors and analogies that help you to better understand the material.

Just by putting together the guide, you will find that you are learning the material. Selecting and sorting from your notes, deciding what is helpful, creating timelines or concept maps (linking the various important concepts together, similar to a mind map) helps you to make choices, think about the material and better order it in your mind. While you're learning, you're forming what are called "neural hooks", to hang the material on. Instead of having a linear mass of facts and numbers, you have linked information in a way that you understand it, which is far more useful to you when preparing for your exam.

Another addition to your study guide can be other guides - for instance, subjects like law, literature, business, accounting have numerous guides available to help you better grasp the material. Instead of relying entirely on the guides - use them as a jumping off point, as well as a gut check. The guide can be a good place to start. Take the topics and make them your own, perhaps coming up with your own examples to understand the concepts better for technical subjects; or for literature courses, starting with the themes given in the guide, ask yourself what other themes appeared in the novel or play. Try to focus on finding guides and material that help you with your weaknesses (see chapter 7). For instance, if you are studying English literature, and you have specific trouble with the themes and symbolism of the novels in the course, but know the plot and characters really well, gather additional material on the thematic aspects of each novel, and try to find questions that concentrate on those elements.

Again I'm suggesting that rather than relying completely on the guide, use it to help you deepen your learning by making the material your own. Also, you can use other available study materials to yield more practice questions (try to get questions of the type likely to appear in your test, i.e. MCQs, or short questions, or essay questions). Add these questions to your personal study guide, forming your own question bank, from which to practice. If you start the process early enough, you can spread out the practice over time, ideally correcting your errors and getting more proficient with each practice session.

You can also use the guides available as a gut-check, a way to double-check that you have studied all the important concepts and that you understand everything. The simple language of a guide can be a good place to start to understand topics you are struggling with, and they usually have examples that may be clearer than your textbook or other reading material.

Once you have created a study guide for each course, you are ready to start preparing for your exam. Before jumping in blindly, create a plan for getting through the material, making sure to space out the work as much as possible (see tip #24). Break your plan into weekly and daily goals, so that it is more manageable. Make sure you set aside time to fill any gaps in your knowledge and understanding of specific concepts. Once you have done that, the best way to really learn the material and be well-prepared, is to test yourself on it.

Tip #35

Go Test Yourself

Most students, including me, fall prey to the habit of simply reading and re-reading their notes, or the chapters of a book, thinking that by becoming familiar with the work they will be able to remember it in the exam. Unfortunately, this is a time-wasting strategy. You will have to remember the information needed under exam conditions, which is a completely different process from simply understanding the material and becoming familiar with it. Yet the strategy most students use is to read something, highlight the important points, and read it again before the test. This is really inefficient and takes up a lot more study time, with a lot less to show for it.

In order to be able to recall the material on demand, you need to internalize the information, which as explained in chapter 6, only happens when you actively engage with it. Research into the way our brain works has shown that testing yourself, which requires your brain to pull up the information needed in the same way you would during the exam, causing the neurons to fire in certain ways, which strengthens the pathway to that information. Numerous studies have found that this is the most effective way to learn. Any strategy that requires you to actively engage with the material, organizing it and recalling it on your own, has been shown to be many times more effective as a study strategy than more passive techniques. The concept of *deliberate practice* stated earlier (see tip #24) indicates that any technique that makes you 'reach' for the correct answer, make a mistake and then correct your mistake, will make you far more likely to remember this information when taking a test on it later.

Create Personalized Quizzes

As you can see, a great way to learn the material for your exams is to test yourself on it. This should, in fact, be your primary exam preparation strategy. Reading and re-reading your notes over and over, hoping that magically you will remember it all on test day, is incredibly inefficient, but a popular strategy nevertheless because it takes less effort. It's harder (and more demoralizing) to check whether you really know the material, then to read it over and over and just hope you do know. Testing yourself requires focus and concentration, and it's actually hard to do it for long periods of time, the way that students typically study for exams, cramming at the last minute. Luckily, you don't need to – there's a better way.

Remember those study guides you made for yourself? Gather those, and any additional material you may have - questions banks, practice exams, flashcards, even online tests on your subject. Spread out the review sessions over several days, depending on how much material you have and how important the test is. If preparing for a mid-term, you might only need two or three days. If prepping for a competitive exam like the SAT or GMAT, you might need weeks.

Basically, once you have understood the material - the concepts you need to define, the problems you need to solve - the next stage is to ensure that you remember them. Using test questions from sample papers, study guides, from the textbook and even ones you make up yourself -- test yourself, writing out the answers or explaining them out loud to yourself, and see how many questions you get right. How you do this depends on the kind of test - is it primarily essay-based, short answers / multiple-choice or problem-based? There are different strategies for each.

Multiple Choice Questions / Short Answers

While tests that are mostly based on providing one-word or

phrase answers, or multiple choice questions (MCQs), seem like they are easy to study for, that might be misleading. Professors like these formats because they are easy to set and correct, but in order not to make them less rigorous, they like to throw a few curveballs. In my experience, the difficulty of questions arise in not just the teacher testing you on whether you have memorized the right dates or all the terminology, but also in checking to see if you have understood the tricky or subtle aspects of the material. Thus, they might test you on terms that are similar or often get confused for one another, or opposites - these can be confusing when presented in MCQ format. For instance, you might get confused between debit and credit. Some Professors like to pick their questions from the footnotes of books, or from appendices or other parts of the material most students would be tempted to skip. (For more advice on how to deal with this, see tip #36.)

The way to effectively prepare for these tests is to pay special attention to terminology, definitions, processes (example in biology or chemistry) or laws (physics and economics). These are ripe areas for questions. Try to find past exam papers, and any question banks that are available for your topic. Also check for solved practice tests available on the internet.

If you're studying for a standardized test, there are dozens of books and other prep material available for students. Unless you sign up for an expensive prep course, it can be overwhelming to know how exactly to approach the mammoth task of preparing for such a test. I would suggest a two-pronged approach. Where material has to be memorized, such as vocabulary or definitions, create flashcards and revise these often, whenever you have a spare moment. You can carry the cards with you and revise on public transportation, standing in queues, and even while out for a walk (be careful of your steps!). I prepared for the vocabulary component of the GRE exam by writing out words and their meanings on index cards, and tested myself while on walks in the park opposite my house. My study methods clearly paid off, because I scored in the 99th percentile for the verbal exam.

Where you have to learn or revise skills, such as solving math problems, you need to learn how to solve each problem of a type. Typically there are a few types of math problems (this also applies to other quantitative exams), and once you have understood how to do one of a type, you can usually do similar ones. (For more detailed advice on solving problems, see below.)

This is only the first part of your revision strategy. The second part is practicing and testing yourself. Your test prep book will provide dozens of examples. Early in your study prep, make practicing as many questions as possible the main focus of your study time. Initially you will be doing untimed practice, getting familiar with different variations in the questions or types of problems. Make sure you do the problem on your own first, and then check the solution - this gives you instant feedback. Closer to your test date, start to practice timed tests. These are available both for free and purchase online for many standardized tests, and the more practice you have under time pressure, the better you will perform.

Lest you think from all this that you have to spend hours and hours preparing, while it is important to put in the time, it's also about what you do with that time. When you don't have many extra hours, use the time you do have by spending more of it from the beginning of your test prep practicing and testing yourself. Keep track of your efforts - are you improving your percentage of correct answers? Take timed tests and see whether you're getting a better score each time. Make a note of the questions you get consistently wrong and go back and revise those. This enables you to get better faster.

Quantitative or Problem-Based Exams

As discussed above, the best approach for preparing for a test requiring you to solve problems during an exam, whether a standardized or another kind of test, is to work through as many test prep materials as you can (a variety of questions ensures you get a wide range and varying levels of difficulty of problems). Check online sources, and apps and games that are available for the test - anything that approaches studying for the test differently (see tip #30). Variety keeps it interesting, so there will be more incentive for you to spend the time needed practicing.

Start with ensuring that you know how to do the worked-out problems from class and from your textbook. Can you do all the homework problems? Practice doing these (examples from the textbook and class, and the homework problems) without the answers in front of you. Go through these problems, and see if you can solve them without mistakes or getting stuck. The ones you are having problems with, just keep a note of them and try them again in your next session, again making a note of the ones you get wrong. Keep repeating till you get all of them right without needing to glance at the solution. This *deliberate practice* ensures that you focus more of your attention on what you're getting wrong, and correcting your errors ensures you improve your grades faster.

Ideally, you would be practicing through the term, and not leave this to the last minute – science and math courses can't be learned in a day or so. If you have been practicing, then in the days before the test, just do a few selected problems from each topic to confirm you can do it correctly, and then go through sample tests provided or extra ones online if available. Doing problems like those you will be tested on is the best way to practice, and if you can do them timed, even better. Doing a sample exam under timed conditions can be a great way to test your level of preparedness for the test.

Check the requirements with your instructor to determine whether there are specific guidelines for how to present the answers. As far as possible, show all your thinking and steps, and even if you're not sure of the final answer, show as much as you can, as you can often get partial credit. This applies to all tests involving working out problems - the more you show the effort you made, and the more clearly you set out the path you took to arrive at your answer, the more credit you can receive even if you got stuck at a particular point or made a calculation error and got the final answer wrong.

Essay-Based Exams

Essay-based exams usually appear in courses which assigned a lot of reading. You would presumably have done the reading and taken good notes. If your notes aren't already thematically arranged, now is the time to do so. Bring the different articles and chapters focusing on one topic together – and try to organize the ideas. What would you say about it on an essay question in the exam? If you have sample exams – use that as a guide to see what sort of questions are asked, and to check how many questions you would be expected to answer. Calculate how much time you have for each question. There is only so much you can write in 45 minutes.

The technique for preparing for essay-based exams is similar to that discussed above. The format and unique aspects of the essay will change depending on the specific exam, but the importance of practice remains just as important.

There are guidelines and sample model answers available for the essay portion of many tests. This is typically the most nerve-wracking part of the test, probably because it is ambiguous, and we generally feel nervous about writing. But don't worry, for most exams you're not being tested on whether you write like Dickens or Shakespeare, the aim is to convey the necessary content, or in some way demonstrate that you have mastered a certain set of skills. Prep books or your instructor will list these skills, and give you tips on how to structure your essay so that you hit the points that examiners typically want to see. The tricky part is getting used to writing in this structure and molding it to the content of what you need to say on a given topic. That's why practicing writing essays on topics from sample past exams, both timed and untimed, is so crucial.

You might be facing a mountain of notes and reading, wondering how you will remember it all for the exam. Try to organize a flow of arguments and ideas about each topic on the course. For instance, a course on Middle East politics might focus on oil, elections, and demographics (among other topics). Create a mind map or an outline of how you would present the arguments and analysis from your readings and lectures (and your own thoughts – which you must make clear are separate from others' ideas), for each of those topics. Practice re-creating the outlines or maps from memory. If you can recall the key 5 - 6 ideas or arguments that you want to present in the essay, you might find the specific details are also attached in your mind, and even if you can't remember everything, the crucial elements will be there.

Once you have organized your material and created your outlines, you could also pick a few sample questions to practice writing about. You obviously won't be able to grade your essays, but it is still valuable practice to hone your thinking and organizing skills as you mentally go through the material you have learned and put your ideas forward systematically. Pick questions that are the most likely to be included (see tip #37), and if the question appears on the actual exam, count yourself lucky and prepare to write a logical, well-thought out answer that will flow more smoothly because you have already practiced it.

How I Increased My Test Scores and Aced My High School Exams

In high school, when studying for my 10th grade board exams, I had to learn a lot of material. A friend of mine who completed her exams the previous year gave me some of the books she had used to prepare, which included several question banks - dozens of tests and practice exams subject-wise, with their solutions.

Once I had studied the topics from the textbooks, I spent a lot of time going over the practice tests. I would try to answer the questions closed-book, then correct them from the solutions given. Many of the questions referenced obscure details that I hadn't picked up on just from reading the textbooks, some even referenced material that I hadn't come across before. The questions were sourced from actual previous years' question papers, so they were exactly the kind of questions that would appear on the exam. By practicing doing exactly what I would have to do on the actual exams (see tip #33), I became more confident in my ability to take the actual exams. By the time I gave the final exams, I didn't really feel nervous, having taken so many practice exams. In fact, many of those obscure questions I prepared for appeared on the test, and I was able to answer them due to my thorough preparation, acing almost every paper.

Although I stumbled upon this technique in high school, but I didn't know truly how powerful it was until many years later when I studied the research. In fact, there were some years when I failed to apply this method, instead laboriously reading and re-reading my material. Why is it that we keep resorting to passive study habits? Because testing yourself is hard work. It's easier to just re-read vocabulary lists, or try practice problems with the solution in front of you. Trying to recall the definition of a term from memory, or writing the solution to a problem is harder, because you have to work hard to remember the required information and go through the steps to answer. Research has shown that recalling something from memory, is metabolically heavy, i.e. it takes a lot of energy for your brain. Reading information, on the other hand, is relatively easier in energy terms. Our bodies and minds are lazy, we like to conserve energy. You will have to actively decide to allocate your study time to quizzing yourself, and may find you can only do this for an hour or so. It is mentally taxing work, but it's the most efficient way to prepare. Try it and see the difference in your grades.

Tip #36

Analyze Your Past Exams

A crucial strategy to improve your grades is to analyze the tests you have already taken in each course. This is best done when you've gotten your results and papers back from your teacher. This is a huge opportunity for feedback to improve your grade, because it helps you target your exam prep to your specific weaknesses and improve them. It is important to know why you did badly in a previous test to know where to focus on for the next one. Even if the topics are slightly or completely different, you should still get a good idea of what to work on.

If you don’t have any past exams in this course to rely on, use turned in homework assignments as a gauge. On the other hand, if you have tests where you don’t know where you went wrong, or what your weak areas are, make an appointment with your instructor to get feedback. They will usually be able to point you quickly towards the areas you need to spend more time on, and may even give you valuable pointers on how to approach the next test. Working on the areas where you are weak or having the most trouble, can make a big difference in your grades as you will increase the efficiency of your study time by focusing it where it can make the most difference.

Find Patterns To Your Mistakes

After the first test of the course, when you receive your paper back with a grade and any comments, go through the paper, noting the mistakes and where you lost points. Get a high-level feel of it initially - did you get mainly the short answers wrong, or lose points on the essays? Did you get entire problems wrong, or did you make tiny calculation errors? Once you make a list of the areas you got wrong, try to figure out a pattern. This will be the blueprint for your study sessions for the next exam. Are there specific areas of the course that is giving you trouble? Try to isolate what elements you really need to beef up for your next test.

Maybe you need to spend more time analyzing the graphs in the textbook - because that's where you tripped up. Or you need more time with your flashcards, because you forgot crucial definitions. Or better time-management, because you ran out of time during the exam, or didn't have enough time at the end to go through your work and catch the errors.

Also use this opportunity to check the relationship between your exam questions and your study guide. For instance, were most of the problems similar to the problem sets you practiced or were they much harder? Maybe they were taken from the sample problems in the textbook - in which case you should plan to go through the relevant chapters in your textbook, solve the problems and get help from the TA or Professor before the next exam. Maybe the short questions were taken from really obscure points in the reading - which means you need to make extra time to go through the reading closely.

This analysis can make all the difference in your grades - no one can know everything related to the course - the successful students are those who usually pay more attention to what matters for the assessment, which differs for each course.

Transforming My Grade in Management Finance

I really struggled with one of my courses in graduate school - there was so much material to get through, all of which was extremely complex and totally new to me. The course didn't have any homework assignments, the grades were based on four exams spaced throughout the course. Unfortunately, despite studying as hard as I could, I bombed the first exam. So did many others, who then dropped the class. But I needed the course and had to find a way to drastically improve my grades. Going over the first test, I realized I had difficulty with some of the trickier multiple choice questions, which were drawn from obscure points in the material. I had also messed up on many of the problems, specifically the ones on topics I was conceptually weak in.

I went through the course material more closely, practicing the sorts of questions I found most difficult. I also looked for additional practice problems elsewhere. The biggest study aid was an optional practice exam booklet that the Professor had mentioned was available to purchase, but that I had initially overlooked. The booklet was divided into quarters, in the same way our tests were, with one sample exam for each quarter. For each test subsequently, I prepared and went over the material and notes, but made sure to leave enough time to go over the sample tests. I did them as a closed-book test, and then checked the answers, going through each a couple of times.

It turned out to make all the difference - I raised my score by almost 30% in the second test, and then continued to get even higher grades in each subsequent test, even as the material got harder, receiving a 96% for my final exam. I had improved so much and so quickly, even the Professor asked me what I had done differently.

Tip #37

Listen For Clues From Your Professor

This is a tip that shouldn't take much time, but can yield a lot of results with little effort. Each teacher has their own unique quirks at marking assignments and setting exam papers. If you can start to see patterns in their behavior, or analyze what they say in class, you can get pointers that will help you in knowing what topics are most likely to be on the test, or how to best approach the preparation.

Being able to know what topics are more likely to appear on the exam helps because you are usually not going to put equal effort into every topic, especially when you have time constraints or a lot of choice on the exam. With exams that are essay-based, you may need to write three essays that are chosen from six given questions on the exam. Ideally, there are at least more than three topics that you have prepared for well and know how to answer. But how do you know what topics will appear from the several that you were introduced to in the course?

Knowing what topics are more important isn't just useful in reducing the number of topics to focus on, but also in the weightage of questions. Topics that are deemed more important may form the basis of more advanced or harder questions or count for more points.

Some Professors give you a hint - either explicitly, in which case note it down and highlight it in your notes, or implicitly, by emphasizing certain topics, or returning to them over and over. In my Islamic law class, the Professor usually repeated her exam questions each year, so practicing the previous years' papers were crucial. Even though the paper usually never changed, the year I took the class, I noticed there was a topic the Professor seemed very interested in, more than usual, and she kept referring to it. When she was asked by a student whether it would be on the exam, she said no. However, I had a strong feeling it would, and prepared that topic especially. Sure enough, it was on the exam, and I was able to write a well-thought out response.

An important point to mention here is that this isn't something to obsess over or spend a lot of time on. I'm not suggesting you stalk or hound your teachers for tips on the exam topics. Just be attentive and note down anything that seems relevant. And make sure to prepare properly for the exam regardless, not over-relying on predicting the topics.

Tip #38

Make Time for Extra Credit Work

Professors sometimes give you optional assignments for extra credit, or sometimes just additional material for extra practice. This extra work on top of everything else you have to do may seem like it should go at the bottom of your to-do list, but that may not be the best thing. Here's why.

If it's an extra assignment, instead of automatically deciding not to do it, glance through it and determine how long it is, what is required, etc. It may be ridiculously hard, and you might think that even attempting it is pointless. However, just trying it might teach you something, maybe showing you exactly which topics in your course you're unclear about conceptually - and remember this information is golden, because knowing your understanding gaps, and eliminating as many of them as possible is one of your primary study goals. Trying the extra credit work, even if you don't get it right, helps you improve your understanding and knowledge of the subject, because it's a form of *deliberate practice.* You are taking on a challenge that is currently beyond you and struggling to improve your ability. Regardless of the outcome, you are subtly improving your skills in that course.

It could also signal to your instructor that you're serious about your grades, and that may have a payoff somewhere down the line where you didn't expect it. Even though we like to think of our teachers as fair and logical, they are human too, and if they perceive you to be a serious student, they could be more lenient if you did poorly on an assignment with some subjectivity in the grading, need an extension for some reason, or some other scenario where showing that you are a together student who has time for extra credit can make a difference.

I'm not, however, suggesting you devote hours and hours of time to this. It is possible the assignment is intentionally difficult.

Or the math is beyond you. Or there is some other reason why you might not be able to do it perfectly. Just give yourself a time limit – say two to three hours at the most, spread out over at least a couple of study sessions. You give it your best shot, and then turn in whatever you have - no matter how meager that turns out to be. And be sure to show all your thinking, all the possible options you came up with. It might seem lame to turn in a half-done assignment, but remember, it is optional. Which means most students won't bother to hand anything in at all, and so just by trying you're standing out. And you never know what could come of it.

The other way this could play out - you are given additional optional material to go through. This is different from supplementary reading that you probably get every week on most humanities and reading intensive courses. I'm referring here to a one-time, one-off additional assignment of material. It could be a book or film that ostensibly provides context. Again you may be tempted to ignore this, but I suggest that you don't. In my Middle East politics class, we were encouraged to watch a film that provided context on one of the class topics. The final exam had a very simple question from the film, which counted for a few points.

The additional material could also be extra practice questions, or sample exams. While this seems to be crucial for test prep, students sometimes ignore this extra material thinking they will get to it after completing the review of the syllabus and all their notes. But as invariably happens, if you don't plan to include something in your prep plan, other things that you "may get to", never get done. These optional extra materials could really improve your test scores and understanding of the material (see tip #36).

Tip #39

Prepare For Exam Day

There are several aspects to properly preparing for an exam, other than actually studying for it. Students who routinely get good grades actually have well-developed exam routines that they don't even consciously think about, like professional athletes. On the other hand, those who are nervous about exams, or think they are resigned to average grades greatly underestimate the fact that taking an exam is not just about how much you know or how many hours you put in studying, it's equally about how you put across this information during the exam.

Advance Preparation

Many students are completely disorganized when they turn up for exams - needing to rush around borrowing a pen, pencil, eraser, whatever. Don't be one of these students - it adds to your own stress, and disturbs others. Being prepared may only save you a few minutes, but saves you much more in equilibrium. It's like the advice to arrive early before a job interview. Besides its one of the ways to act like a top student without too much effort - just plan for everything you might need the night before an exam and bring it - extra pens, pencils, sharpener, eraser, your ID if needed, some snacks if they are allowed (nothing that crunches too much - chocolate bar or protein bar is probably most ideal), water and any special implements such as a calculator. This way you can be confident that you have everything you need.

Part of this preparation is being properly hydrated (but not so much that you need to keep heading to the bathroom), and eating an appropriate snack beforehand. You want to make sure you eat something, but not so much that you're uncomfortably stuffed, or falling asleep. The best strategy is to eat something light and nutritious, with protein to keep you full, and not too many simple carbs, because it can cause a high and then a crash of energy. You can keep a non-crunchy snack if you're allowed one. I used to keep small chocolate biscuits during my 3-hour exams in law school, they were like a treat for getting through each section of the exam, and a quick energy and mood boost.

If you start to feel really nervous at any time, take some slow, deep breaths, and feel your heart rate coming down. It's important to be as calm as you can, because you will actually perform better. It is, however, okay to feel a little bit of nervousness, it keeps you sharp. If you have prepared well, relax and do your best. This isn't the only exam you will ever take, and like any other skill, you can get better at taking exams over time.

Planning Your Time

When the paper starts, or even in advance if you know the format, plan out your time. Most students rush into answering the questions, but this is a mistake. Running out of time, or failing to answer all the questions can be a fatal mistake, costing you points unnecessarily. Look through the exam and allocate time to each question, or set of questions. Do this based on how much they are worth and the type of question. For instance, if you have four essays of equal weightage to answer in 3 hours, break the time equally, and give yourself 40 minutes of writing for each essay. This will leave a 20 minute buffer. If you have a short question section, worth 40 points, and three essays or problems worth 20 points each, to complete in 2 hours - then spend 30 minutes on the short question section, and 25 minutes on each essay question. This leaves you with 15 minutes of buffer. Once you have allocated your time for each question, stick to it ruthlessly. If your 25 minutes for the first essay is up, and you still have a few points to make, leave adequate space in your answer book, and move on to the other questions, returning to it when you have time. Leave a note to yourself on the points you intend to include, in case you are worried about forgetting. This is where the buffer comes in. Take a few minutes from this buffer time after you have completed all the questions to return to the ones you left partially answered.

The other reason for the buffer is to leave a little extra time for the beginning and end of the exam. Before you start to write, read through the instructions carefully, going over each page, so that you know what questions to answer. Friends of mine have failed to turn a page of the exam paper, missing questions on the final page. Or sometimes, you are given options, and you must answer a set number from the options. It has happened in the past that I wrote one more essay than I needed to, because I didn't read the instructions carefully. That not only causes you added stress, you don't do the best job possible if you're spreading yourself thin answering extra questions. Reading the instructions is very important, and if you don't understand exactly what you need to do, ask. You don't want to waste time doing extra work or missing out by not reading the paper closely.

At the end, after you have answered all the questions, try to leave 5 - 10 minutes at the very least, a little more for technical exams, to go over your work. Check that you've answered everything you were supposed to, that you've labeled your answers clearly, and that your personal information is filled out. For technical papers, go back over your work and check your work to see that you haven't skipped any steps, or made any obvious errors. This step always leads to corrections or additions, therefore it's crucial that you don't skip it.

The reason for the complicated math of splitting up the questions by time is that while the questions may have equal weightage in terms of points, you may find certain questions easier to answer than others, or have more to say. Allotting the time in advance prevents you spending one hour answering the question you find easy and like, and then having only 10 minutes left for each of the remaining questions. You're better off coming back to add more once you've attempted each question.

Planning Your Answer

Before you begin an essay question, spend a couple of minutes planning your answer. It may be tempting to just jump in, but a quick plan helps you make sure you hit all the points you need to. It only needs to be a few words, not a formal outline. Do whatever works for you - I sometimes created mini-mind maps, especially if I couldn't remember every point or in the right order - or I would re-create the maps I made to study certain topics on the exam sheet, to ensure I remembered everything. The plan helps when you're writing - in case you forget a point, it is right there. Also, you will be able to check how much time you have, and depending on how many points you still need to cover, abbreviate some of your thoughts, or write faster. The time it takes to plan will more than make up for it in helping you to give your best on the exam.

**

If you have studied using the tips given in this book, you should be improving your grades with each test and course. As you practice these concepts, you will find yourself becoming a better student, calmer, less stressed and it will look to others as if you're effortlessly doing well in school. You still need to work hard, but by working in such a way as to make the best use of your mind and ability to learn, you will find yourself accomplishing more than you ever thought you could. All the best!

Epilogue

Jason and Grace Get As

Jason loves playing basketball, and hanging out with his friends, listening to music and strumming his guitar. He doesn't particularly like school or studying: his big dream is to play college basketball, and then get recruited to play professionally.

In order to get an athletic scholarship, Jason knows that he needs to maintain a B average at least. Earlier in the year, his grades were really poor, but he started to change some of his study habits, and he slowly saw his grades improving.

Jason has basketball practice most days, and likes to spend time with his friends as well, so he doesn't have a lot of time to study. To maximize his time, he wakes up early on Sundays. After a hearty breakfast with his family, he sits down with his planner and makes a list of everything he needs to get done that week. He notes down all the assignments and reading, as well as any tests coming up in the next few weeks, that he can start to prepare for.

Once Jason has a list, he prioritizes it, and plans when he will work on what. He knows this is a tentative list, as things will change. Some work will take longer than planned, and some days he will be so tired from practice, he won't have the willpower to stick to his plan. That's why he keeps a buffer, planning a little more time than he needs for larger assignments.

He starts to work on the first item on his list - after first putting his phone on silent mode. After an hour of reading and taking notes on his assigned reading for history, he gets up to stretch, and drink some water. Deciding that his pace on the work is flagging, he switches to his math homework, and is able to get half the assignment done in 90 minutes. Before finishing up for the day, he makes a quick list of things he needs to remember for the next day and what he plans to study on Monday.

During the week, by referring to his daily and weekly lists, Jason gets most of his homework completed during school hours, in breaks between classes and rising early before school. By working in focused chunks of time, he is more efficient. He even manages to start creating the study guide for a test that is coming up in 3 weeks. He also pays attention in class and takes good notes, knowing that it will save him study time later.

He usually has basketball practice after school, after which he is too tired to do much serious work. He uses the time before dinner to organize his notes and papers, and do the lighter, background reading from his courses. He also goes through his class notes to see if there are any large gaps, which he makes a note of, to ask his teachers or classmates. When he has tests coming up, he uses this time to make flashcards and put together a study guide, with sample questions. Realizing that getting in enough recall practice before a test is important, Jason spends several early morning study sessions in the weeks before a test, learning the material and testing himself without looking at the answers. After dinner, he catches up with his friends for a short while, before going to bed early. Friday evenings and most of Saturday, Jason hangs out with his friends, plays basketball and practices some new songs on his guitar. On particularly busy weeks, Jason devotes an hour or a maximum of 90 minutes after breakfast on Saturdays, catching up with his assignments.

By spreading out his work, and doing it while he is fresh, in focused sessions without any distractions, Jason is able to do his best work. He plans what he needs to study, and uses each session productively. Also, instead of spending his time passively reading the text and highlighting, he takes focused notes and tests himself on the material. He also takes practice tests and goes through sample quizzes when they are available. This way he is confident that he will finally be able to tackle the exams and do well. His hard work pays off, and Jason improves his grades significantly, even getting an A$^+$ in history, a subject that gave him so much grief earlier.

**

Grace is a quiet, shy girl. She loves reading, and can always be seen with her nose in a book. She gets the highest grades in creative writing and her essays are frequently read out in class by the teacher and passed around for the other students as an example of "model writing".

She secretly dreams not of being a writer, as everyone naturally assumes, but a doctor. She hopes to one day become a surgeon, and work for Doctors Without Borders. However, Grace has problems with math and science classes, struggling with the quantitative material. When her guidance counselor advises her to either improve her grades or change her goal to something "more realistic", Grace is determined to find a way to accomplish her dream of studying medicine.

She first takes a hard look at her test results and makes a list of exactly which topics she finds difficult. She gets books that simplify the material she is struggling with, as well as finds extra practice tests and quizzes. She creates a plan to go through the extra material on weekends, going to the library near her house to concentrate. For certain subjects she needs to go back to the early topics, when she first started having difficulties. She breaks up her study time, practicing problems from different textbooks and topics, so that she doesn't get bored and learns what methods to apply for each type of problem.

When she finds a concept difficult, she tries to break apart the topic, really trying to understand each small component, using metaphors and analogies to better grasp the concept. Grace also goes to her teachers with any problems that she just can't understand on her own, or tries to find videos online explaining the topic. It is difficult at first, and sometimes she feels like giving up. But seeing how hard she is working, her friends and family encourage Grace, saying that they are proud of her for sticking to her plan.

As she gets more confident with practice problems, she starts to attempt harder and harder problems. Eventually, as she practices more and starts to see the links between the different concepts she is studying, Grace gets better grades at school, and even begins to really enjoy math and science. She can see that she understands the material better, and is doing well in her practice tests. Finally, the day comes when Grace gets her first A⁺ on a math test. She is really excited, but it is only the beginning on her path towards fulfilling her dreams.

Notes

Chapter 1: Adopting The Right Attitude

Tip #1

"A famous research study was conducted": Carol S. Dweck, *Mindset: The New Psychology of Success*. New York: Random House, 2006.

Tip #2

"A recent article in the New York Times": Julie Scelfo, "Suicide on Campus and the Pressure of Perfection", 27 July 2015, http://www.nytimes.com/2015/08/02/education/edlife/stress-social-media-and-suicide-on-campus.html?_r=0

Statistics on suicide from NGO Active Minds - http://www.activeminds.org

"Friends' lives, as told through selfies": Quoted in Julie Scelfo, "Suicide on Campus and the Pressure of Perfection".

"difference to how much we learn": Carol Dweck, *Mindset.*

"those with an overly perfectionist outlook": Tal Ben-Shahar, *The Pursuit of Perfect: How to Stop Chasing Perfection and Start Living a Richer, Happier Life*, McGraw-Hill, 2009.

"an opportunity for receiving feedback": Ibid, p.10.

Tip #3

"A short list of famous dyslexics": Details taken from this link - "Famous People with the Gift of Dyslexia", http://www.dyslexia.com/famous.htm.

"This definitely made my course work more challenging": Email correspondence with Kimberly Erskine, 20 July 2015.

"Kimberly experimented with different hearing aids": I took some details of Kimberly's story from her blog post - “Confessions of A Def Deaf Girl — My Story”, 27 October 2014, https://confessionsofadefdeafgirl.wordpress.com/2014/10/27/confessions-of-a-def-deaf-girl-my-story/

"When your determination changes": Quote from Dr. Daisaku Ikeda, http://www.ikedaquotes.org/attitude/attitude104?quotes_start=14.

Tip #4

"Allow some time for serendipity": This idea is adapted from Frans Johansson, *The Click Moment: Seizing Opportunity in an Unpredictable World*, Penguin, 2012.

Chapter 2: Nourishing Your Mind And Body

Tip #5

The connection between energy and performance taken from the following book - Tony Schwartz, Jean Gomes, and Catherine McCarthy, *The Way We're Working Isn't Working: The Four Forgotten Needs That Energize Great Performance*, Simon and Schuster, 2010.

"research shows that taking proper breaks": Tony Schwartz and Catherine McCarthy, “Manage Your Energy, Not Your Time”, *Harvard Business Review*, Oct 2007. https://hbr.org/2007/10/manage-your-energy-not-your-time.

The discussion on focus and diffused modes was informed by Barbara Oakley, *A Mind for Numbers: How to Excel at Math and Science (Even If You Flunked Algebra)*, New York: Jeremy P. Tarcher / Penguin, 2014. This is an oversimplified explanation, see the book for more details about these modes of thinking.

The idea that taking a break or doing something different can help you to reach more insights taken from multiple sources, but for a good explanation, see Daniel J. Levitin, "Hit the Reset Button in Your Brain," *The New York Times*, August 9, 2014.

"work expands so as to fill the time available for its completion": Also known as Parkinson's Law, as it was first stated by Cyril Parkinson, in an essay published in 1955.

Tip #6

Research on how sleep affects our memory taken from multiple sources: Benedict Carey, *How We Learn: The Surprising Truth About When, Where, and Why It Happens*, New York: Random House, 2014; John Medina, *Brain Rules: 12 Principles for Surviving and Thriving at Work, Home, and School*, Pear Press, 2008 and Barbara Oakley, *A Mind for Numbers: How to Excel at Math and Science (Even If You Flunked Algebra)*, New York: Jeremy P. Tarcher / Penguin, 2014.

Understanding of how learning happens while we sleep: James Gallagher, "Sleep's memory role discovered", BBC News, 6 June 2014, http://www.bbc.com/news/health-27695144. Also, Guang Yang et al. "Sleep promotes branch-specific formation of dendritic spines after learning", *Science* 344, 1173 (2014).

The statistic about sleeping within four hours of learning from Josh Kaufman, *The First 20 Hours: How to Learn Anything...Fast!*, Penguin, 2013.

Research on the function of sleep in removing toxins from: John Hamilton, "Brains Sweep Themselves Clean of Toxins During Sleep", NPR All Things Considered, October 17,

2013. Also, Xie, Lulu, Hongyi Kang, Qiwu Xu, Michael J Chen, Yonghong Liao, Meenakshisundaram Thiyagarajan, John O'Donnell, et al., "Sleep Drives Metabolite Clearance from the Adult Brain", *Science*, 342, no. 6156 (2013): 373-77.

My information on the creative habits and rituals of writers and artists taken from Mason Currey, *Daily Rituals: How Artists Work*, New York: Alfred A. Knopf, 2013.

Tip #7

The connection between exercise and creativity explored in many articles, and this one explains it quite well: Gretchen Reynolds, "Want to be More Creative? Take a Walk." *The New York Times,* April 30, 2014.

Research on the benefits of exercise on brain function: John Medina, *Brain Rules: 12 Principles for Surviving and Thriving at Work, Home, and School*, Pear Press, 2008; Leo Widrich, "What Happens To Our Brains When We Exercise And How It Makes Us Happier", *Fast Company,* 2014, http://www.fastcompany.com/3025957/work-smart/what-happens-to-our-brains-when-we-exercise-and-how-it-makes-us-happier

Richard Branson's productivity advice: Ciara Conlon, "How to Supercharge your Productivity the Richard Branson Way", http://www.lifehack.org/articles/productivity/how-to-supercharge-your-productivity-the-richard-branson-way.html

Tip #8

Research on the link between nutrition and focus, concentration and energy levels: Mark Hyman, *Ultrametabolism: The Simple Plan for Automatic Weight Loss,* Simon and Schuster, 2008 and Mark Hyman, *The Blood Sugar*

Solution: The Bestselling Programme for Preventing Diabetes, Losing Weight and Feeling Great, Hodder and Stoughton, 2012. Also see, Leo Widrich, "How the Food You Eat Makes You More (or Less) Productive", *Lifehacker.com*, 19 Oct 2012. http://lifehacker.com/5953060/how-the-food-you-eat-makes-you-more-or-less-productive

Tip #9

Research on the effect of caffeine: Kevin Purdy, "What Caffeine Actually Does To Your Brain", http://lifehacker.com/5585217/what-caffeine-actually-does-to-your-brain. To understand the science behind how caffeine works on our brain, see Stephen R. Braun, *Buzz: The Science and Lore of Alcohol and Caffeine*, Oxford University Press, 1997.

Research on the correlation between dehydration and cognitive performance: A Adan, "Cognitive performance and dehydration", J Am Coll Nutr. 2012 Apr; 31(2):71-8.

Chapter 3: Organizing Your Study Life

Tip #11

For a more thorough understanding of working memory, see: Barbara Oakley, *A Mind for Numbers: How to Excel at Math and Science (Even If You Flunked Algebra)*, New York: Jeremy P. Tarcher / Penguin, 2014; David Rock, *Your Brain at Work: Strategies for Overcoming Distraction, Regaining Focus, and Working Smarter All Day Long*, Harper Collins, 2009.

To understand why we cannot evaluate priorities in our heads, and to learn how the limits of our brain affect our cognitive processing, read this excellent book: David

Rock, *Your Brain at Work: Strategies for Overcoming Distraction, Regaining Focus, and Working Smarter All Day Long*, Harper Collins, 2009.

"Sunday Ritual": Cal Newport, "Follow a Sunday Ritual", http://calnewport.com/blog/2007/09/26/follow-a-sunday-ritual/.

"ski trip right at the time of a midterm exam": Email conversation with Margaret Thompson Reece, PhD.

Tip #12

For more information on prioritizing, planning and understanding the limits of our working memory, see David Rock, *Your Brain at Work: Strategies for Overcoming Distraction, Regaining Focus, and Working Smarter All Day Long*, Harper Collins, 2009.

Chapter 4: Getting The Most From Your Study Time

"Research shows that sessions of focused work": See for more on how focused work helps increase learning - Barbara Oakley, *A Mind for Numbers: How to Excel at Math and Science (Even If You Flunked Algebra)*, New York: Jeremy P. Tarcher / Penguin, 2014.

Tip #14

Statistics on lost productivity: Ned Smith, "Distracted Workers Cost U.S. Businesses $650 Billion a Year", http://www.businessnewsdaily.com/267-distracted-workforce-costs-businesses-billions.html (accessed July 20, 2015); Jennifer Shore, "Social Media Distractions Cost U.S. Economy $650 Billion", November 3, 2012, http://mashable.com/2012/11/02/social-media-work-productivity/.

Research on social media use by college students and link to GPAs: Steven W. Glogocheski, Ed.D. "Social media usage and its impact on grade point average and retention: An exploratory study to generate viable strategies in a dynamic higher education learning environment". Dissertation submitted to St. John's University, School of Education and Human Services, 2015.

"the truth is that we don't multitask": For research on multi-tasking, see John Medina, *Brain Rules: 12 Principles for Surviving and Thriving at Work, Home, and School*, Seattle: Pear Press, 2008.

"every status update you read on Facebook": From a New York Times article on multi-tasking and the science of attention - Daniel J. Levitin, "Hit the Reset Button in Your Brain", *The New York Times,* August 9, 2014.

Research on interruptions, distraction and loss of productivity: Cole, W., et al., "The Multitasking Generation", *Time* 167 (2006): 50-53; Jennifer Shore, "Social Media Distractions Cost U.S. Economy $650 Billion", November 3, 2012, http://mashable.com/2012/11/02/social-media-work-productivity/.

The concept of *flow state* and its benefits comes from Mihaly Csikszentmihalyi, *Flow: The Psychology of Optimal Experience*. New York: Harper and Row, 1990.

Working in focused blocks: Daniel J. Levitin, "Hit the Reset Button in Your Brain", *The New York Times,* August 9, 2014; David Rock, *Your Brain at Work: Strategies for Overcoming Distraction, Regaining Focus, and Working Smarter All Day Long*, Harper Collins, 2009.

Tip #15

Notion of 'pseudo-work': Cal Newport, *How to Become a Straight-A Student: The Unconventional Strategies Real College*

Students Use to Score High While Studying Less, Crown/Archetype, 2006, pp. 15-16.

"A novelist who dramatically increased her daily output": Rachel Aaron, *2k to 10k: Writing Faster, Writing Better, and Writing More of What You Love*, 2012.

Tip #17

Details on the rituals of Woody Allen and Maya Angelou taken from Mason Currey, *Daily Rituals: How Artists Work*, New York: Alfred A. Knopf, 2013.

"Research has also shown that studying in different environments": Benedict Carey, *How We Learn: The Surprising Truth About When, Where, and Why It Happens*, New York: Random House, 2014.

Chapter 5: Beating Procrastination

Tip #19

Perfectionism and its effects on productivity: see generally, Hillary Rettig, *The 7 Secrets of the Prolific: The Definitive Guide to Overcoming Procrastination, Perfectionism and Writer's Block*, Infinite Art, 2011 and Julia Cameron, *The Artist's Way: A Spiritual Path to Higher Creativity*, New York: Penguin, 1992.

Advice on breaking down projects and working on easier aspects first: Hillary Rettig, *The 7 Secrets of the Prolific: The Definitive Guide to Overcoming Procrastination, Perfectionism and Writer's Block*, Infinite Art, 2011, section 5.4.

Tip #21

Pomodoro technique - see http://pomodorotechnique.com/ for more about the technique and how to apply it.

Tip #22

Research on habits and routines comes from Charles Duhigg, *The Power Of Habit: Why We Do What We Do In Life And Business,* New York: Random House, 2012.

"The goal should be achievable and have the right level of challenge": Email conversation with Dr. Naoisé O'Reilly and Marie P. D. O'Riordan, 16 July 2015.

Research on the links between pleasure and video games: David J. Linden, "Video Games Can Activate the Brain's Pleasure Circuits", *Psychology Today,* Oct 25, 2011, https://www.psychologytoday.com/blog/the-compass-pleasure/201110/video-games-can-activate-the-brains-pleasure-circuits-0.

Tip #23

"Structured procrastination": John Perry, "Structured Procrastination: Do Less, Deceive Yourself and Succeed Long-Term", originally published in 1995, reprinted here: http://www.structuredprocrastination.com/.

Chapter 6: Studying Effectively

Tip #24

To further understand the concept of working memory and its limitations, see David Rock, *Your Brain at Work: Strategies for Overcoming Distraction, Regaining Focus, and Working Smarter All Day Long*, Harper Collins, 2009.

To understand the process of chunking and how it helps us to learn better, see Barbara Oakley, *A Mind for Numbers: How to Excel at Math and Science (Even If You Flunked Algebra)*, New York: Jeremy P. Tarcher / Penguin, 2014.

"Deliberate practice" is a term first coined by researcher K. Anders

Ericsson in his ground-breaking paper on the subject of elite performance: K. Anders Ericsson, Ralf Th. Krampe, and Clemens Tesch-Romer, "The Role of Deliberate Practice in the Acquisition of Expert Performance", Psychological Review 1993, Vol. 100. No. 3, 363-406.

An excellent book on deliberate practice, which he refers to as "deep practice": Daniel Coyle, *The Talent Code: Greatness Isn't Born. It's Grown. Here's How,* New York: Random House, 2009. Also on this topic, see Geoff Colvin, *Talent is Overrated: What Really Separates World-Class Performers from Everybody Else*, Penguin, 2008.

"It entails considerable, specific, and sustained efforts": K. Anders Ericsson, Michael J. Prietula and Edward T. Cokely, "The Making Of An Expert", Harvard Business Review, Jul-Aug 2007. https://hbr.org/2007/07/the-making-of-an-expert

"It is only human nature": Quote from Sam Snead cited in ibid.

Research on spaced repetition and spacing out study time: Barbara Oakley, *A Mind for Numbers: How to Excel at Math and Science (Even If You Flunked Algebra)*, New York: Jeremy P. Tarcher / Penguin, 2014; Benedict Carey, *How We Learn: The Surprising Truth About When, Where, and Why It Happens*, New York: Random House, 2014.

Research on optimal timing of spaced sessions and the *spacing effect*: S. K. Carpenter, N.J. Cepeda, D. Rohrer, S.H.K. Kang, & H. Pashler, "Using spacing to enhance diverse forms of learning: Review of recent research and implications for instruction", *Educational Psychology Review, 24*(3), 369-378, 2012. doi: 10.1007/s10648-012-9205-z

Cal Newport's theory of intensity and the benefit of study sessions spread out over time: Cal Newport, "The Straight-A Gospels: Pseudo-Work Does Not Equal Work", http://calnewport.com/blog/2007/07/26/the-straight-a-gospels-pseudo-work-does-not-equal-work/

Research on interleaving: Barbara Oakley, *A Mind for Numbers: How to Excel at Math and Science (Even If You Flunked Algebra)*, New York: Jeremy P. Tarcher / Penguin, 2014; S. K. Carpenter, N.J. Cepeda, D. Rohrer, S.H.K. Kang, & H. Pashler, "Using spacing to enhance diverse forms of learning: Review of recent research and implications for instruction", *Educational Psychology Review, 24*(3), 369-378, 2012. doi: 10.1007/s10648-012-9205-z; Doug Rohrer, Robert F. Dedrick, and Kaleena Burgess, "The Benefit of Interleaved Mathematics Practice Is Not Limited to Superficially Similar Kinds of Problems", *Psychonomic Bulletin & Review* in press (2013).

Tip #25

"washes over us like a warm bath": Daniel Coyle, *The Talent Code: Greatness Isn't Born. It's Grown. Here's How,* New York: Random House, 2009.

"The most important thing to do is to pay attention in class": Email conversation with Macromanolis Panagiotis (Enterhydra.gr), 17 July 2015.

"A really good strategy is to compare notes with your classmates": Email conversation with Margaret Thompson Reece, Ph.D. (http://www.medicalsciencenavigator.com/), 17 July 2015.

"Re-writing and condensing notes a second time really drills it in": Email correspondence with Rob Mayzes, 17 July 2015.

"Research shows that anything that organizes the information": J Dunlosky, K. A. Rawson, E. J. Marsh, M.J. Nathan, & D.T. Willingham, "Improving students' learning with effective learning techniques: Promising directions from cognitive and educational psychology", *Psychological Science in the Public Interest, 14* (1), 4-58, 2013.

Cal Newport's QEC (Question-Evidence-Conclusion) method: Cal

Newport, *How to Become a Straight-A Student: The Unconventional Strategies Real College Students Use to Score High While Studying Less*, Crown/Archetype, 2006.

"it is best to organize and process your notes in class as much as possible": See generally Michael Friedman, "Notes on Note-Taking: Review of Research and Insights for Students and Instructors", Harvard Initiative for Learning and Teaching, http://hilt.harvard.edu/files/hilt/files/notetaking_0.pdf

Tip #26

"Learning style": The three broad learning styles are visual, auditory and kinesthetic.

For general information on learning styles, see "Three Learning Styles", http://blc.uc.iupui.edu/Academic-Enrichment/Study-Skills/Learning-Styles/3-Learning-Styles for a brief description of the three main learning styles and some tips for each style.

The examples of creating a website or app for programming, or reading through balance sheets for learning accounting from my email conversation with Macromanolis Panagiotis, 17 July 2015.

Tip #27

For more general tips on approaching your writing assignments with more ease and less stress, see this excellent book on writing: Hillary Rettig, *The 7 Secrets of the Prolific: The Definitive Guide to Overcoming Procrastination, Perfectionism and Writer's Block*, Infinite Art, 2011.

Tip #28

Details on Sue Grafton's use of a journal in writing her books: Sue

Grafton, "The Use of the Journal in Writing a Novel", in eds. Meg Leder, Jack Heffron, *The Complete Handbook of Novel Writing*, Writer's Digest Books, 2002, pp. 193-203.

Use of a quotes or source document: Cal Newport, *How to Become a Straight-A Student: The Unconventional Strategies Real College Students Use to Score High While Studying Less*, Crown/Archetype, 2006, pp. 174-182.

Chapter 7: Tackling Difficult Subjects

Tip #30

"supplying the missing pieces": Scott Young, "How to learn subjects that are above your level", http://www.scotthyoung.com/blog/bootcamp-2015-day-5/.

Yale Environmental Law course: Professor John Wargo, "Environmental Politics and Law", https://www.youtube.com/playlist?list=PL84DCD72C5B5DC403

For more information on language practice, see the excellent resources available on Benny Lewis' site: http://www.fluentin3months.com

Tip #31

"after all, the Professors are there to help you": Email conversation with Macromanolis Panagiotis, 17 July 2015.

"If you failed to understand a concept": Email conversation with Margaret Thompson Reece, PhD, 17 July 2015.

"Dig beneath your feet, there you will find a spring": Quote from Dr. Daisaku Ikeda, philosopher and founder of the Soka Schools and Universities. http://www.ikedaquotes.org/attitude/attitude110.html?quotes_start=7

Chapter 8: Revising For Exams

Tip #33

"Athletes and other elite performers": Details on Tiger Woods' practice from Geoff Colvin, *Talent is Overrated: What Really Separates World-Class Performers from Everybody Else*, Penguin, 2008.

"Neural hooks": Barbara Oakley, *A Mind for Numbers: How to Excel at Math and Science (Even If You Flunked Algebra)*, New York: Jeremy P. Tarcher / Penguin, 2014.

Tip #35

"Research into the way our brain works": Benedict Carey, *How We Learn: The Surprising Truth About When, Where, and Why It Happens*, New York: Random House, 2014.

Research on recalling from memory: David Rock, *Your Brain at Work: Strategies for Overcoming Distraction, Regaining Focus, and Working Smarter All Day Long*, Harper Collins, 2009.

Bibliography

A Adan. "Cognitive performance and dehydration". J Am Coll Nutr. 2012 Apr; 31(2):71-8.

Barbara Oakley. *A Mind for Numbers: How to Excel at Math and Science (Even If You Flunked Algebra).* New York: Jeremy P. Tarcher / Penguin, 2014.

Benedict Carey. *How We Learn: The Surprising Truth About When, Where, and Why It Happens.* New York: Random House, 2014.

Cal Newport. *How to Become a Straight-A Student: The Unconventional Strategies Real College Students Use to Score High While Studying Less.* Crown/Archetype, 2006.

-- "The Straight-A Gospels: Pseudo-Work Does Not Equal Work". http://calnewport.com/blog/2007/07/26/the-straight-a-gospels-pseudo-work-does-not-equal-work/

-- "Follow a Sunday Ritual". http://calnewport.com/blog/2007/09/26/follow-a-sunday-ritual/.

Carol S. Dweck. *Mindset: The New Psychology of Success.* New York: Random House, 2006.

Charles Duhigg. *The Power Of Habit: Why We Do What We Do In Life And Business.* New York: Random House, 2012.

Ciara Conlon. "How to Supercharge your Productivity the Richard Branson Way". http://www.lifehack.org/articles/productivity/how-to-supercharge-your-productivity-the-richard-branson-way.html.

Cole, W., et al. "The Multitasking Generation". *Time* 167 (2006): 50-53.

Daniel Coyle. *The Talent Code: Greatness Isn't Born. It's Grown. Here's How.* New York: Random House, 2009.

Daniel J. Levitin. "Hit the Reset Button in Your Brain". *The New York Times*, August 9, 2014

David J. Linden. "Video Games Can Activate the Brain's Pleasure Circuits". *Psychology Today*, Oct 25, 2011, https://www.psychologytoday.com/blog/the-compass-pleasure/201110/video-games-can-activate-the-brains-pleasure-circuits-0.

David Rock. *Your Brain at Work: Strategies for Overcoming Distraction, Regaining Focus, and Working Smarter All Day Long*. Harper Collins, 2009.

Doug Rohrer, Robert F. Dedrick, and Kaleena Burgess. "The Benefit of Interleaved Mathematics Practice Is Not Limited to Superficially Similar Kinds of Problems". *Psychonomic Bulletin & Review* in press (2013).

Frans Johansson. *The Click Moment: Seizing Opportunity in an Unpredictable World*. Penguin, 2012.

Geoff Colvin. *Talent is Overrated: What Really Separates World-Class Performers from Everybody Else*. Penguin, 2008.

Gretchen Reynolds. "Want to be More Creative? Take a Walk." *The New York Times,* April 30, 2014.

Guang Yang et al. "Sleep promotes branch-specific formation of dendritic spines after learning". *Science* 344, 1173 (2014).

Hillary Rettig. *The 7 Secrets of the Prolific: The Definitive Guide to Overcoming Procrastination, Perfectionism and Writer's Block*. Infinite Art, 2011.

J Dunlosky, K. A. Rawson, E. J. Marsh, M.J. Nathan, & D.T. Willingham. "Improving students' learning with effective learning techniques: Promising directions from cognitive and educational psychology". Psychological

Science in the Public Interest, *14* (1), 4-58, 2013.

James Gallagher. "Sleep's memory role discovered". BBC News, 6 June 2014, http://www.bbc.com/news/health-27695144

Jennifer Shore. "Social Media Distractions Cost U.S. Economy $650 Billion". November 3, 2012, http://mashable.com/2012/11/02/social-media-work-productivity/.

John Hamilton. "Brains Sweep Themselves Clean of Toxins During Sleep". NPR All Things Considered, October 17, 2013.

John Medina. *Brain Rules: 12 Principles for Surviving and Thriving at Work, Home, and School.* Pear Press, 2008.

John Perry. "Structured Procrastination: Do Less, Deceive Yourself and Succeed Long-Term". originally published in 1995, reprinted here: http://www.structuredprocrastination.com/.

Josh Kaufman. *The First 20 Hours: How to Learn Anything...Fast!* Penguin, 2013.

Julia Cameron. *The Artist's Way: A Spiritual Path to Higher Creativity*. New York: Penguin, 1992.

Julie Scelfo. "Suicide on Campus and the Pressure of Perfection", 27 July 2015, http://www.nytimes.com/2015/08/02/education/edlife/stress-social-media-and-suicide-on-campus.html?_r=0.

K. Anders Ericsson, Michael J. Prietula and Edward T. Cokely. "The Making Of An Expert". Harvard Business Review, Jul-Aug 2007, https://hbr.org/2007/07/the-making-of-an-expert.

K. Anders Ericsson, Ralf Th. Krampe, and Clemens Tesch-Romer. "The Role of Deliberate Practice in the Acquisition of Expert Performance". Psychological Review 1993, Vol. 100. No. 3, 363-406.

Kevin Purdy. "What Caffeine Actually Does To Your Brain".

http://lifehacker.com/5585217/what-caffeine-actually-does-to-your-brain

Leo Widrich. "How the Food You Eat Makes You More (or Less) Productive". Lifehacker.com, 19 Oct 2012. http://lifehacker.com/5953060/how-the-food-you-eat-makes-you-more-or-less-productive

-- "What Happens To Our Brains When We Exercise And How It Makes Us Happier". *Fast Company*, 2014. http://www.fastcompany.com/3025957/work-smart/what-happens-to-our-brains-when-we-exercise-and-how-it-makes-us-happier

Mark Hyman. *Ultrametabolism: The Simple Plan for Automatic Weight Loss.* Simon and Schuster, 2008.

Mason Currey. *Daily Rituals: How Artists Work*. New York: Alfred A. Knopf, 2013.

Michael Friedman. "Notes on Note-Taking: Review of Research and Insights for Students and Instructors". Harvard Initiative for Learning and Teaching, http://hilt.harvard.edu/files/hilt/files/notetaking_0.pdf.

Mihaly Csikszentmihalyi. *Flow: The Psychology of Optimal Experience*. New York: Harper and Row, 1990.

Ned Smith. "Distracted Workers Cost U.S. Businesses $650 Billion a Year". http://www.businessnewsdaily.com/267-distracted-workforce-costs-businesses-billions.html

Rachel Aaron. *2k to 10k: Writing Faster, Writing Better, and Writing More of What You Love*. 2012.

S. K. Carpenter, N.J. Cepeda, D. Rohrer, S.H.K. Kang, & H. Pashler. "Using spacing to enhance diverse forms of learning: Review of recent research and implications for instruction". Educational Psychology Review, *24*(3), 369-378, 2012. doi: 10.1007/s10648-012-9205-z

Scott Young. "How to learn subjects that are above your level". http://www.scotthyoung.com/blog/bootcamp-

2015-day-5/.

Steven W. Glogocheski, Ed.D. "Social media usage and its impact on grade point average and retention: An exploratory study to generate viable strategies in a dynamic higher education learning environment". Dissertation submitted to St. John's University, School of Education and Human Services, 2015.

Sue Grafton. "The Use of the Journal in Writing a Novel". Eds. Meg Leder, Jack Heffron. *The Complete Handbook of Novel Writing*. Writer's Digest Books, 2002.

Tal Ben-Shahar. *The Pursuit of Perfect: How to Stop Chasing Perfection and Start Living a Richer, Happier Life*. McGraw-Hill, 2009.

Tony Schwartz and Catherine McCarthy. "Manage Your Energy, Not Your Time". *Harvard Business Review*, Oct 2007 https://hbr.org/2007/10/manage-your-energy-not-your-time

Tony Schwartz, Jean Gomes, and Catherine McCarthy. *The Way We're Working Isn't Working: The Four Forgotten Needs That Energize Great Performance.* Simon and Schuster, 2010.

Xie, Lulu, Hongyi Kang, Qiwu Xu, Michael J Chen, Yonghong Liao, Meenakshisundaram Thiyagarajan, John O'Donnell, et al. "Sleep Drives Metabolite Clearance from the Adult Brain". Science, 342, no. 6156 (2013): 373-77.

Acknowledgements

This book was something that I have wanted to write for years; in fact, I wrote the very first draft more than 10 years ago. I really enjoyed writing this book, but in some ways it was also one of the hardest for me to write, and I wouldn't have been able to get to the end without lots of help.

Firstly, I want to thank my parents, Ratna and Ashish Mukherjee, for putting up with my ever-changing moods and phone calls complaining about my lack of progress. They inspired me to be curious and to love learning, and supported me even when that curiosity took me in unexpected directions.

I want to thank my friends at the gym, especially Ragamalika Magendar, who provided welcome distractions when I really needed it. I also want to thank the Laguna Park Management Committee -- for their inspired provision of the Reading Room -- where I spent many hours reminding myself of my student days.

I also want to thank Help A Reporter Out for their wonderful service, and the generous individuals who wrote to me with their stories and tips, especially Kimberly Erskine, Rob Mayzes, Dr. Margaret Reece, Macromanolis Panagiotis, Marie O' Riordan and Dr. Naoisé O'Reilly.

About the Author

Geetanjali Mukherjee grew up in India, spending her early years in Kolkata, and then attending high school in New Delhi. She studied law at the University of Warwick, United Kingdom, and further earned a Masters' in Public Administration at Cornell University, USA.

Geetanjali's first book, "Seamus Heaney: Select Poems", is in its 6th edition currently, published by Rama Bros. India. She is also the author of four other books, and writes about creativity and productivity at her blog Creativity@Work. Geetanjali currently lives in Singapore.

Contact the Author:
Email: geetanjalimukherjee.author@gmail.com
Twitter: @geetmuk
Facebook: www.facebook.com/geetumuk

13072718R00129

Made in the USA
Lexington, KY
27 October 2018